MONTREAL'S CENTURY

MONTREAL'S CENTURY

A RECORD OF THE NEWS AND PEOPLE WHO SHAPED
THE CITY IN THE 20TH CENTURY

The Gazette   TRÉCARRÉ

Photographs
Front cover: Nancy Ackerman, Gordon Beck, George Bird, George Cree, John Mahoney, André Pichette, Dave Sidaway, COJO Archives and Gazette Files.
Back cover: Gazette Files.
End papers, title page and opposite page: Gazette Files and Gordon Beck.

Canadian Cataloguing in Publication Data

Main entry under title:
    Montreal's century
    Issued also in French under title: Un siècle à Montréal
    ISBN 2-89249-656-X
    1. Montreal (Quebec) - Pictorial works. 2. Montreal (Quebec) -
History - 20th century. 3. Montreal (Quebec) - Biography

FC2947.37.S5313 1999   971.4'28'00222   C99-941532-8
F1054.5.M843S5913 1999

Editor: Jennifer Robinson
Design: Cyclone Design Communications

ISBN: 2-89249-656-X

Legal deposit, 1999
Bibliothèque nationale du Québec
Printed in Canada

Trécarré acknowledges the financial support of the Government of Canada through the Book Publishing Industry Development program for its publishing activities.

Éditions du Trécarré
Outremont (Quebec) Canada

TABLE OF CONTENTS

FOREWORD

In a dusty room on the fifth floor of The Gazette building on St. Antoine Street are rows and rows of filing cabinets containing thousands of photographs taken since the newspaper first began publishing photos more than 100 years ago.

Back then, photography was in its infant stages and the few photos The Gazette published were usually staged portraits. It wasn't until later that technology would allow newspaper photographers to capture the speed of hockey heroes like Maurice Richard. Colour would come even later – it has been only in the past 20 years that Montreal newspaper photographers have shot in colour and newspapers have published colour photos.

Today, our photographers are armed with the technology to shoot any event, no matter where or how quickly it unfolds. And rather than stuffing prints into filing cabinets as was done for most of this century, newspapers today store images electronically.

To celebrate the end of the century, we at The Gazette and Le Journal de Montréal wanted to share some of our wonderful photos taken over the years. The Gazette's archives contain more than three million photos and negatives, including those taken for the Montreal Star, the Standard and other newspapers that closed down in this century.

The challenge was not in finding historically significant photos, but rather choosing which ones to include in the book. Unfortunately, far too many great photos didn't make it.

Still, we believe the photos that did, coupled with the essays by seven of our most senior writers, reflect a vivid portrait of the city.

We didn't set out to publish a history book, but rather a collection of photos and essays that recall some of the important events and people who have shaped Montreal and the lives of Montrealers in the past 100 years.

Initially, our goal was to use only photos owned by The Gazette or Le Journal de Montréal or for which copyright restrictions have expired. But for various reasons, we had to make a few exceptions.

Many thanks to the Roman Catholic Archdiocese of Montreal for allowing us to publish their pictures of the Eucharistic Congress in 1910.

Many thanks also to the Quebec Archives for giving us access to the COJO Olympic photo collection, to which our photographers contributed in 1976.

Many people have contributed their time and talent to producing Montreal's Century.

Thanks to Gazette publisher Michael Goldbloom, who made the book possible and encouraged our unique collaboration with our collegues at Le Journal de Montréal.

Many thanks go to Gazette librarians, in particular Donna MacHutchin, who compiled much of chronology in the final chapter.

Special gratitude is owed to Hubert Bauch, one of Canada's finest journalists who, in addition to writing two essays, wrote many of the captions for the photographs.

We are especially grateful to Marc Laberge and Gisèle LaRocque at Les Éditions du Trécarré for their guidance and professionalism and to Caroline Desrosiers and her colleagues at Cyclone Design Communications Inc. for their graphic talents and wonderful design and layout.

Thanks to Mark Daly and Russ Peden for copy editing and proof reading the texts.

Finally, to the many talented journalists and photographers, present and past, who have captured Montreal's history as it has unfolded, we owe many thanks and much admiration.

JENNIFER ROBINSON
*Editor of Montreal's Century
and Associate Editor of The Gazette*

Introduction

JOHN **KALBFLEISCH**

I T WAS DECEMBER 31, 1900, a Monday. James Wills, an otherwise obscure employee of the city, found that as operator of the municipal fire-alarm system he suddenly was a personage of some standing. As midnight approached, he was pestered by increasingly frantic telephone calls from citizens anxious to know precisely when the new century would begin. But, secure in the operations room at Montreal city hall, he was not to be deflected. Just as the minute hand touched 12, Wills pulled a lever that activated fire alarms

The first two decades of the 20th century were a period of unprecedented growth in Montreal. The population more than doubled to 618,000 and the city expanded northward beyond Sherbrooke Street. Electric steetcars made travel in winter bearable. The corner of St. Denis Street (looking north) and Laurier Avenue in 1914 didn't have the trendy appeal it had acquired by the end of the century. (GAZETTE FILES)

all over the city, "one round of 12 blows struck for the end of the old and the beginning of the new century."

And so it was. For Montrealers and well nigh everyone else, 1901 was the first year of the 20th century, not 1900.

It's not clear who the first Montrealer of the century was, though it can be noted that on January 3 a woman went into labour on a street-

PREVIOUS PAGES

Only the Victoria Bridge connected Montreal to the South Shore when the century began. It would be 30 years before the Jacques Cartier Bridge, originally called the Montreal Harbour Bridge, would open. It took four years to build – this photo dates from 1928 – at a cost of $18 million.

It's remarkable how much the Montreal of yore prefigures the city today. The 80 bus replaced the 80 streetcar on Bleury and Park Avenue. (GAZETTE FILES)

car on what is now St. Antoine Street. The conductor called an ambulance but it arrived too late. "The number of passengers had been increased by one," it was drolly reported, "but no additional fares were collected."

If James Wills were somehow to awaken today, he'd be astonished by the changes in his city. There is its vastly increased population, as well as its sheer geographic extent from suburbs like Hudson in the west to Repentigny in the east, from Ste. Thérèse, within hailing distance of the Laurentians, south to St. Bruno and beyond. Skyscrapers had begun to appear downtown in 1900, but they were puny – six- and eight-storey affairs – compared with the Sun Life Building, the giant structures put up in the pre-Expo boom and the more recent IBM and Teleglobe towers. And where once there was just a single crossing over the Street Lawrence River

By the mid-1950s, the corner of Ste. Catherine and Peel had become the heart of Montreal's business core and the language – as the apostrophes suggest – was primarily English. Twenty years later, the Parti Québécois government brought in Bill 101 that would change the face of the downtown core to French. (GAZETTE FILES)

from Montreal to the South Shore, now there are a half dozen.

What would Wills think of the speed of machines and people in the streets, the strange noises (Muzak, the muted clatter of a computer keyboard, car horns, jets overhead), the bright lights, especially at night, the casual fashions and manners? Where have the mansions along Dorchester and Belmont streets gone, the stench in the air from the horses and open drains, the ships in the Lachine Canal, the faithful packing the churches on a Sunday?

Yet it's remarkable how much the Montreal of 1900 prefigures the city of today. The tramways had just been electrified, which meant their routes could be extended and new residential neighbourhoods established. No longer did people have to live within walking distance of where they worked; commuting had begun.

Then, as now, new-wave industry was flexing its muscle. Then, it was companies like Dominion Bridge and Canadian General Electric; now, it's Nortel, Ubisoft Entertainment and Bombardier-owned Canadair. Then, the city was home to one of the world's best-known universities, McGill; today, thanks to McGill and its sister institutions Concordia, Université de Montréal and UQÀM, the city continues to breathe rarefied intellectual air.

Something else has persisted: a feeling among Montrealers that the city is special, verging on the unique.

It's easy to see why this was so a century ago. Montreal was the biggest city in the country, its financial, commercial and manufacturing capital, effectively the birthplace of organized hockey, lacrosse and football, the arbiter of social and artistic fashions, a major cipher in the

Styles have evolved but Montrealers still have that kind of panache and love of life that they had when this 1938 photo was taken at the public beach on Ile Ste. Hélène. (GAZETTE FILES)

Canadian political equation. Knowing all this gave Montrealers a certain swagger – or at least the calm self-assurance, the sense of confidence in one's own skin.

Montrealers still have that kind of swagger, that panache – call it what you will – though the reasons for it have shifted to more subtle ground.

In Montreal, it might be said, people have unlocked the secret of living the good urban life. Compared with any other large city you'd care to name, the cost of living is attractive, the streets are relatively safe, you can live downtown, in the distant suburbs or somewhere in between in

equal style, and the traffic is not so outrageous that the city is effectively cut off from the beauties of its surrounding lakes and rivers, forests and fields – or for that matter, those on the mountain. A sense of community life – that is, of life lived in common – emerges from the sidewalk cafés and restaurants that dot every neighbourhood, from extravaganzas like the Tour de l'Île and the Jazz Festival's public concerts, even from shared hardship like digging out from beneath a blizzard.

Like any large city worth its salt, Montreal is cosmopolitan, a gathering place of unnumbered languages and cultures. But almost with-

The horse-drawn buggy was still monarch of Montreal's roads when the century began, but within a generation the city had developed a car-parking crisis. At the turn of the century, Champs de Mars behind city hall was a thriving farmers' market. By 1920 it had been paved over and turned into a parking lot.

out exception, the great cities, cosmopolitan though they may be, are fundamentally monocultural: Paris is French, London and New York are English. Montreal is a rare example – Brussels, perhaps Bombay and Hong Kong are others – of a city that is fundamentally more than that. Diminished though the presence of English may be in Montreal, vast numbers of people in the city nevertheless speak both French and English, have friends and lovers from the other culture, are not averse to living next door to each other. Arguably, French and English rub up against each other in Montreal as two of the world's great cultures do nowhere

else on Earth. And both are enhanced by the presence of so many other cultural communities that share the city.

There are friction burns from time to time, to be sure. But far more than we sometimes acknowledge, as the new century is rung in, there is still excitement, creativity, a sense of being special. James Wills would know the feeling. ◆

Politics and passion

HUBERT **BAUCH**

T here was much fretting in the sunset years of the 20th century about the curse of political uncertainty. Every earnest discussion about the state of *fin-de-siècle* Montreal would inevitably zero in on political uncertainty, and then revolve around the question of how deeply it would drive Montreal into privation and disrepute before the city's political weather cleared for a predictable stretch.

But looking back on a century of politics in Montreal makes it about as hard to envisage a Montreal untroubled by political uncertainty

Sir Wilfrid Laurier, shown here with wife Zoë on their 50th wedding anniversary in 1918, was the prime minister who led Canada into the 20th century. He was the first French Canadian prime minister, and the 15 years he served (1896 - 1911) amount to the longest continuous term in office of any prime minister. Born in the Laurentian hamlet of St. Lin, he studied law at McGill and set up his first practice in Montreal. Though it is the most famous of quotes attributed to him, Laurier never actually said that the 20th century would belong to Canada. (GAZETTE FILES)

PREVIOUS PAGES

Montreal is not the capital of Quebec but it is the crucible of Quebec politics. The landmark cross atop Mount Royal has served as a billboard for political messages, in its own right and on several occasions since its erection in the 1920s by the St. Jean Baptiste Society. The 101 banner was hoisted in 1988 in support of the ban on English commercial signs, which was ruled unconstitutional by the Supreme Court later that year. (GAZETTE – NANCY ACKERMAN).

A common Montreal scene during the 1980 sovereignty referendum. Signs on a balcony proclaim conflicting allegiances among residents of the same block. (GAZETTE)

as it is to picture a world at peace. In practice, political certainty is an inherent contradiction; the only certainty in politics is that sooner or later, things will not go according to plan or precedent. One of the pertinent lessons of Montreal history in the 1900s is that whenever it seemed most certain that the city was assured a rosy future, the prophets of joy were never more mistaken.

It might seem that Montreal had more to celebrate at the dawning of the century than at its dimming, that there was more certainty in the city's prospects than in today's Montreal, which may or may not be part of Canada or of Quebec when the time comes to look back on the 21st century. The Montreal of 1900 was in the full flower of its gilded age as the reigning metropolis of a Canada constituted in large measure to serve Montreal's interests. It was the country's propelling urban dynamo, its capital of industry and its showcase of auspicious wealth – all things that can't be said of Montreal any more. Sir Wilfrid Laurier was prime minister; the premier of Quebec was F.G. Marchand, and the mayor of Montreal was Raymond Préfontaine: all were staunch Liberals and great Canadians. Queen Victoria reigned, as she had for more than half a century, over a British Empire kissed by sunshine since the Napoleonic Wars and in whose bosom Canada preened as its senior dominion. Yet all was not well with Montreal's world even then.

The Gazette account of the 1900 New Year's observance at St. George's Church opposite Windsor Station reported that the urge to celebrate the new century was dampened by a "war cloud" hanging over the country and concern for the "valiant sons of Canada" – some of them Montreal sons – called to arms by Mother Britain to fight in the Boer War. It reported that bells were rung, but not joyous bells: "Today those bells have to send forth their tidings of a new era and the subdued resonance of muffled harbingers instead of clanging them unhindered and unfettered to the rolls of drums of a successful army heralding peace and happiness to all." Montreal's spring that year was marred by three days of rioting in the midtown streets that flared when McGill University students, marching to celebrate a key British victory in the city of Ladysmith in Natal province, collided with French-speaking students demonstrating against the conscription of Canadian soldiers for a British colonial war. By the following January, Montreal was in mourning for the passing of Queen Victoria, and the age of abiding certainties that carried her name. That November, the final bell tolled for yet another era when Sir Charles Tupper, a Montrealer by adoption and the last of the original Fathers of Confederation still bearing the torch of John A. Macdonald, resigned as Conservative party leader after a defeat in the first national election of the new century. (Not for another 80 years would another Tory leader match Macdonald's feat of winning successive majorities, and it would be another naturalized Montrealer, Brian Mulroney.)

Montreal's rising political star at the turn of the century was Henri Bourassa, who had recently bolted the federal cabinet to preach separatism – by which he meant separating Canada from British imperial subjugation, as disturbing a notion in the day as Quebec independence would be half a century later. Upstart Toronto was beginning to crowd Montreal's first-city comfort zone, and there was concern, even in the heyday of the wealthy Square Mile neighbourhood, over the future of the city's English community: in the first two decades of the century, the percentage of anglo Montrealers of British origin declined from fully a third to less than a quarter of the city's population.

While Montreal is no longer the country's biggest and wealthiest city, the Montreal of

Most of Canada's great political orators this century sprang from Quebec, and among these was Henri Bourassa, pictured here at an anti-conscription rally in 1942. Denounced in his time as a subversive rabblerouser and laterally hailed as the avatar of modern Quebec nationalism, he was actually Canadian ahead of his time. In 1910, he founded Le Devoir to promote his causes: Canadian autonomy, British ideals, minority rights, provincial autonomy and public service bilingualism. He lived by the motto on his paper's masthead: Do what must be done. (GAZETTE FILES – MONTREAL STAR)

the year 2000 still ranks as Canada's most interesting city. And it is likely to be so as long as it retains its French-English duality. But this also makes for a volatile political mix, which greatly explains Montreal's perennial uncertainty problem. An interesting town makes for interesting times, both for the better and in the sense

Médéric Martin, Mayor of Montreal, 1914-24 and 1926-28, was Montreal's first "people's mayor" whose strength was his oratory, not his upper class connections. A cigar roller by trade, he began his career as a working class hero, but became increasingly fond of opulent trappings, lavish ceremony and funds of dubious provenance. On this 1920s occasion, he was receiving Romanian royalty – Prince Nicolas and Queen Marie – in the trademark style of his later years. (GAZETTE FILES)

Camillien Houde, here in full platform flight, was "Monsieur Montreal" to some and the "Canadian Mussolini" to others, but he was unquestionably Montreal's most flamboyant mayor. His career in office spanned four decades (1928-32; 1934-36; 1938-40; 1944-54) and survived a four-year internment for inciting draft evasion during World War II. (GAZETTE FILES)

The brief reign at city hall of Henry Ekers from 1906 to 1908 – the mayoral term was two years in his day – was a signal of changing times in Montreal, and growing French power. Ekers was Montreal's last English mayor, and with him passed the traditional English-French alternation in the mayor's chair that had endured since the city's incorporation in 1832. A brewing magnate, his name is remembered mostly for the eponymous brand of ale his brewery produced. (GAZETTE FILES)

Montreal city hall was ruled for most of the century by a succession of three mayors of towering legend. The third, Jean Drapeau, had a penchant for grandiose public monuments, but was prominently modest in his personal indulgences. He made a fetish of driving himself even when he had a chauffeur on staff, not only because he enjoyed driving around his city, but, as he once told an interviewer, he didn't want the neighbours saying, should he ever lose an election: "Look, he's got to drive his own car again." (GAZETTE FILES)

of the ancient Chinese malediction that wishes interesting times on one's worst enemy. Unsettled times are always of greater interest to historians than times of stability – for the same reasons a photo of a house fire rates bigger front-page play if there are flames shooting through the roof than if there's just a lot of smoke. So even as it slipped to No. 2, Montreal continued making more history, and banner headlines for that matter, than any other Canadian city.

In the realm of municipal politics, Montreal showed a distinct preference for interesting mayors, and a persistent capacity to produce them. For most of this century's years, city hall was ruled by a succession of three mayors of towering legend who were the incarnation of the city's character in their respective eras. All three were populists with princely ambitions; all three

were ardent French-Canadian nationalists and all three shepherded Montreal through interesting times in its civic development. They were singularly given to extravagant public works and all three left office under a cloud of opprobrium. They were Médéric Martin (1914-24, 1926-28); Camillien Houde (1928-32, 1934-36, 1938-40, 1944-54); and Jean Drapeau (1954-57, 1960-86). Martin was Montreal's first "people's mayor," where his predecessors were conventionally anointed by the city's commercial upper crust. A cigar maker by trade who still carried his card from the local cigar rollers' union even as he wore the mayor's chain, Martin drew his power from Montreal's burgeoning francophone working class, which by the century's second decade had the numbers to swing civic elections. After Henry Ekers (1906-08), Montreal never had another English mayor,

When war was declared, many francophone Montrealers, urged on by such leaders as Camillien Houde, opposed conscription and Canada's participation in the Allied war effort. In this 1941 photo, hundreds rallied against conscription in Champs de Mars. (GAZETTE FILES)

where until then a rule of English-French alternation had been observed. When Martin came to office, Montreal's late-19th century industrial boom was going bust, now that the country's major railways, whose construction built Montreal's greatest fortunes, had been laid from coast to coast, and most of the choice local real estate snapped up. World War I was breaking out, and while this proved good for Montreal business, it shattered the city's social peace as English and French divided bitterly over conscription to the point of brawling in the streets, a pattern repeated a quarter century later during World War II. In what would also be a familiar Montreal pattern, Martin's enthusiasm for public works put the city so deeply in hock that the banks were given charge of its books. His final days in office were blighted by a typhoid epidemic for which civic health authorities were found highly to blame, and the revelation that a brewery producing a line of "bière

Martin" was paying the mayor a penny on the six-pack to rent his name.

Camillien Houde's ascent coincided with the onset of the Great Depression, followed a decade later by the upheavals of the second Great War. A man of copious girth and earthy demeanour, Houde is widely esteemed as the city's most entertaining public figure of the century, at once the most dearly beloved and most furiously denounced of Montreal mayors. In the manner of great Montreal mayors, his gift was for showmanship, not accounting; for a period after Houde's third term, the city fell under provincial trusteeship.

Typical of the style that endeared him to the city's proletarian masses was his reputed aside to King George VI as they rode through streets lined with cheering Montrealers during the 1939 royal visit that marked the first time a reigning monarch set foot in the city: "Some of that is for you, your majesty."

Thousands of other Montrealers volunteered to fight the Nazi forces in Europe. This photo of men lined up to register was taken in September 1939. (Gazette files – Montreal Standard)

Houde made history during the World War II years by becoming the only Canadian mayor ever declared an enemy of the state after he prominently advocated draft dodging, for which he was clapped in an internment camp from 1940 to 1944. The ultimate measure of Houde's populist magic was his re-election as mayor within months of his release. He would endure another decade before scandal caught up with him: while the 1954 report of the "Caron vice probe" into the city's thriving prostitution and gambling rackets did not directly incriminate the mayor, it starkly exposed a civic administration rotted through with corruption. He was succeeded as mayor that fall by the inquiry's lead counsel, a crusading young Montreal lawyer with political ambitions of his own.

Jean Drapeau went on to win seven more elections, and stamped his name on a Montreal era that eclipsed even Houde's extraordinary reign. He was not just Montreal's longest-serv-ing mayor, his 28 years in office made him the most durable of Canada's major political figures this century. In Drapeau's time, Montreal became a truly modern city, a city of skyscrapers, expressways and underground concourses, a city of global distinction and world-class carnivals. He introduced the party system to Montreal politics, and presided over Montreal's fully elected city council. (Until 1962, a third of its seats were by appointment.) Where Martin and Houde were champions of Montreal's French-Canadian toiling class, Drapeau was a product of the city's emergent francophone and Quebec nationalist middle class, whose aspirations he flattered with his politics of grandeur.

As befits its greatest mayor, Drapeau also presided over some of the city's most interesting times – both the most glorious and the most turbulent of Montreal times, from Expo fanfare to Olympic folly. He was typical of Montreal-style mayors, only more so. He was a charmer

"The Olympics can no more have a deficit than a man can have a baby" will endure as Jean Drapeau's most memorable quote. It was a colossal miscalculation. At the closing ceremonies in 1976, it was clear Montrealers would be paying for the "Big Owe" for many years to come. (COJO ARCHIVES)

and a tyrant, a dreamer and a schemer, imperiously unconstrained by budgetary shortcomings. His darkest hour came when the provincial government seized control of his Olympic project after its cost estimate had multiplied more than tenfold. It was failing health, not electoral defeat or scandal, that finally drove Drapeau from office. He was re-elected even after it was proven that high-level incompetence and corruption had fuelled the skyrocketing Olympic construction costs. Once again, the mayor was not personally incriminated, but some of his closest associates were. Drapeau would have preferred to be remembered for his

Jean Drapeau (left), mayor of Montreal, 1954-57; 1960-86. The greatest of Montreal mayors, for better or for worse. (GAZETTE – GEORGE CREE)

operative slogan: "There are no problems, only solutions." But it is his magisterially inadvised estimate of the Olympic bottom line that endures as his most memorable quote: "The Olympics can no more have a deficit than a man can have a baby." By latest estimate, Montrealers will be paying off the mayor's colossal miscalculation into the second decade of the new century.

Montreal is not the official capital of Quebec, but it is the crucible of Quebec politics. It is where the leading-edge ideas and evolutionary movements come to the fore, where all its factions are resident and where push comes to shove. Montreal is where changes happen in Quebec politics; what happens in Quebec City are merely the attendant formalities. As Montreal inexorably lost its early-century entitlement as

Canada's metropolis to Toronto, it grew steadily into a new vocation and identity as Quebec's metropolis. This is perhaps the single biggest Montreal political story of the century – what was in effect a French reconquest of the city. The renaming of Dorchester Boulevard after René Lévesque in the late 1980s was perhaps its supreme symbolic affirmation, but it was heralded as early as 1901 with the proclamation of Parc Lafontaine, which few today remember was previously Logan Park. First political power and later economic power passed from the city's once-dominant anglo commercial oligarchy to a rising new francophone elite, a transition that inevitably made for politically interesting times.

The greater part of Canada's political attention and energies during the latter part of the century were wrapped around the so-called "Quebec question" – how to accommodate a resurgent French Quebec in an increasingly English Canada – and as Quebec's metropolis, Montreal was the natural ground-zero for the constitutional wars of the past four decades. Since Montreal is home to more than 80 per cent of Quebec's English population, it was also the epicentre of four decades of language conflict. The major language bills passed in Quebec City during the period, from Bill 22 to Bill 101 to Bill 178 to Bill 86, were dictated by Montreal factors and were felt most acutely in Montreal.

Two of Canada's leading historians recently compiled the 25 "events that shaped the country" for the national newsmagazine, Maclean's. Of the dozen that occurred since 1960, seven either took place in Montreal or had a prominent Montreal connection. These include Quebec's Quiet Revolution; Centennial year and Expo 67; the 1970 FLQ crisis; the Canada-Soviet summit hockey series of 1972; the 1982 constitutional patriation and Charter of Rights; the Canada-U.S. free trade accord in 1988 and the 1989 École Polytechnique massacre of 14 female students by a deranged lone

gunman, the worst single-day mass murder in Canadian history, committed in the name of anti-feminism.

The Quiet Revolution is commonly dated from 1960, when Jean Lesage's housecleaning Liberals stormed the seats of power in Quebec, bringing a formal end to the postwar era in Quebec politics named for its longest-serving premier, Maurice Duplessis, a time since proscribed in the shorthand of collective memory as "La grande noirceur," the great darkness. But its clarion sounded in Montreal a dozen years before when a group of Montreal artists and intellectuals came forth with the "Refus Global," a virulent manifesto that sweepingly repudiated the venally hidebound Duplessis regime and the stifling overlordship of the Roman Catholic church in Quebec's affairs of state, a holdover from the reign of the Bourbons. The FLQ was almost wholly a Montreal phenomenon, from the first Westmount mailbox bombings of the early '60s to the October kidnapping crisis of 1970 that provoked the only peacetime declaration of the War Measures Act. The protracted constitutional struggle leading up to the 1982 patriation – via the first sovereignty referendum in 1980 – boiled down in large measure to a titanic running debate between two Montrealers, Pierre Trudeau and René Lévesque. Arch-federalist Trudeau was first elected prime minister in 1968, the year Lévesque became the founding leader of the separatist Parti Québécois; the debate goes on without them, but not much of substance has been added to what they said in their time. Free trade came to pass during Brian Mulroney's term as prime minister, with critical backing from Montreal's nouveau corporate elite.

The Montreal time this century that shines brightest in the civic memory is the summer of 67, when it seemed that the magic of Expo would make everything turn out all right for Montreal, for Quebec and for Canada. "Stand

Maurice Duplessis had no inkling, as he celebrated his fourth provincial election win, that the man with the microphone behind him would someday succeed him as premier. But then neither did René Lévesque back in 1952, when he was making a name for himself as a Radio-Canada reporter. (GAZETTE FILES - MONTREAL STAR)

The Quiet Revolution dated from 1960, when Jean Lesage's Liberals were swept to power. Here, Lesage unleashes a blast of rhetorical thunder during a 1966 campaign speech in Montreal. It was to be his last election. His Liberal "Équipe du tonnerre" was rumbled out of office that spring by a resurgent Union Nationale under Daniel Johnson. (GAZETTE FILES)

Like father, like sons. Premier-elect Daniel Johnson Sr. poses proudly with his family on election night in 1966. In a dynastic feat unmatched in Canadian politics, not one but both his sons would follow him into the premiership, Pierre Marc (right) in 1985 and Daniel in 1994. The Johnson women are wife Reine and daughters Diane (left) and Marie (right). Johnson père was felled by a fatal stroke midway through his term. (GAZETTE FILES)

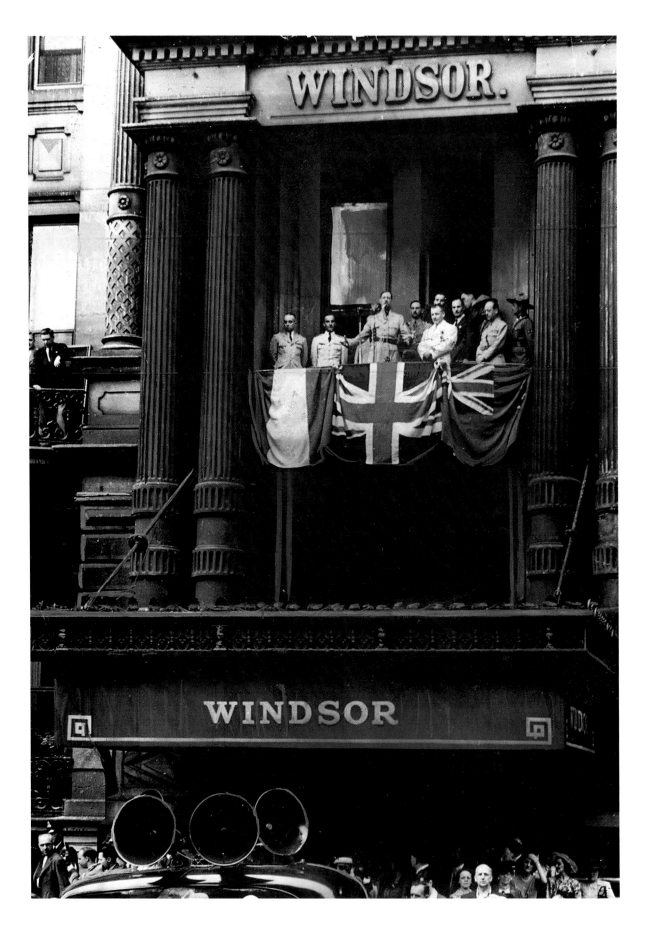

When Charles de Gaulle spoke from the balcony of the Windsor Hotel during a 1944 visit to Montreal (left) he had nothing but praise for Canada, and thanks for its role in the recent liberation of France from Nazi occupation. His gratitude had waned by the time of his next visit in 1967 (above) when he spoke from a different balcony, this time at city hall, and delivered a different message. His cry of "Vive le Québec libre" dampened the feel-good atmosphere of the Expo 67 summer and galvanized Quebec's rising separatist movement. (GAZETTE FILES – MONTREAL STAR)

up Canada and take a bow!" crowed the Gazette front page when the Expo gates opened. "You've built the greatest world exhibition the Earth has ever known. You've confounded the prophets of gloom, converted the cynics and proven that we can make dreams as big as our land come true." But for all its glowing promise, Expo summer proved to be only a false dawn that faded before the leaves turned that fall. No one had dreamed the political highlight of the summer would be the president of France fomenting Quebec separatism from the balcony of Montreal city hall. (Less remembered is the first time Charles de Gaulle spoke from a Montreal balcony, at the Windsor Hotel in 1944.

Then, he was copiously grateful to Canada for its stellar role in the recent liberation of France from Nazi occupation; it was "Vive le Canada" and "Vive la France," and nothing about "le Québec libre.") The following summer is most memorable for the street fighting: in June, separatist rowdies stoned the reviewing stand at the St. Jean Baptiste Day parade where Pierre Trudeau was in prominent attendance; in August the St. Léonard school riots erupted, and worse would shortly follow. From the dream bath of Expo, Montreal was plunged into its contemporary age of uncertainty. Perhaps the most hopeful trend in Montreal's civic life at the close of a turbulent century is that violence has gone

One of the century's most memorable riots erupted on St. Jean Baptiste Day in 1968 when police and separatist demonstrators clashed in front of the reviewing stand on Sherbrooke Street East where Pierre Trudeau and Jean Drapeau (seated on dais) were ensconced (above). Dozens were arrested (below). The image of Trudeau standing his ground under a rain of stones and bottles helped boost the Liberal vote in the next day's federal election, Trudeau's first as prime minister. (Gazette files)

out of fashion as a means of political expression. For many of the city's years, street riots were as ingrained a Montreal institution as St. Jean Baptiste parades, and for a time in the radical '60s the two were combined. The city has seen religious riots, conscription riots, language riots, labour riots, student riots and hockey riots. Montreal might still be the national capital, as it was in 1848, had a Montreal mob not torched the house of Parliament that year. The urge to run ape in the streets is perhaps not entirely purged from the Montreal character, as the Stanley Cup riot of recent memory attests. But for more than a quarter century now, there has not been a Montreal riot worthy of the name in aid of a political cause. There is no saying for certain that there will never be another, but Montreal politics have become progressively

Montreal's most destructive street rioting this century erupted on October 6, 1969, the day Montreal's police and firemen staged a one-day strike, leaving the streets unguarded against rampaging mobs that burned and looted at will. This photo shows an car torched outside the Murray Hill garage, one of the principal targets of politically motivated rioters that day. (GAZETTE FILES)

The sign said it all. Raymond Lemieux, leader of a movement to abolish English schools in Quebec, whipped up his followers before one of a rash of language riots in north-end St. Léonard in 1968. Loosely translated, the sign says: "If you want an English school, move the hell to Ontario." (GAZETTE FILES)

The most notorious figures of the 1970 October Crisis were the Rose brothers, Paul (left) and Jacques (above), shown here being led to their arraignment where they were charged with kidnapping and murdering Quebec labour minister Pierre Laporte. For all their defiant bravado at their arraignments, it was the beginning of the end of the FLQ. The backlash of public revulsion against the October Crisis violence and its forceful renunciation by the independence movement's political leadership, rang down the era of separatist terrorism. (GAZETTE – TEDD CHURCH AND AUSSIE WHITING)

less sectarian, less ideologically driven and less class-based. There are still vestiges of the old Two Solitudes, but there is a growing sense among Montrealers of all backgrounds and persuasions of being in the same boat. The outlook is still clouded by uncertainty, but on its present political course, the good ship Montreal is drawing closer to the spirit of its official motto – Concordia salus – which loosely translated from Latin means: A town that rows together will never go under. ◆

The October 1970 kidnappings of British diplomat James Cross and Quebec labour minister Pierre Laporte, seen in the photo above with his wife a few months before he was murdered, led to the imposition of the War Measures Act. Laporte's body was found in the trunk of a car (right) in St. Hubert. (GAZETTE FILES)

Hundreds of Canadian Forces troops were called in to secure Montreal's streets after the War Measures Act was proclaimed during the 1970 October Crisis. It was a salvation for some, as this photo (above) outside the Drummond Street Salvation Army headquarters suggests, but damnation for many others. Few Montrealers were indifferent about the army's presence in the city. (GAZETTE–TEDD CHURCH AND GARTH PRITCHARD)

Two of Canada's political titans of the century were Montrealers – Prime Minister Pierre Trudeau and Premier René Lévesque. The great Canadian constitutional debate of the late century has revolved largely around their difference of opinion about the relationship Quebec should have with the rest of Canada. (GAZETTE FILES)

A stunning victory. René Lévesque's Parti Québécois swept to power on November 15, 1976, marking one of the century's major turning points for Montreal and Quebec. (GAZETTE - MICHAEL DUGAS)

It wasn't always easy, but René Lévesque — unlike Péquiste premiers who followed — attempted on several occasions to reach out to Montrealers of all stripes. The PQ had just adopted its French only language laws in 1977 when Lévesque met with West Islanders (above). (GAZETTE - LEN SIDAWAY)

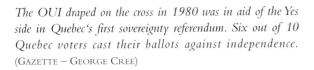

The OUI draped on the cross in 1980 was in aid of the Yes side in Quebec's first sovereignty referendum. Six out of 10 Quebec voters cast their ballots against independence. (GAZETTE – GEORGE CREE)

Montreal has always been the epicentre of Quebec's language conflicts, from Bill 22, to Bill 101, to Bill 178, to Bill 86. English Montrealers (left) protested the Bourassa government's use of the notwithstanding clause in 1989 to maintain French-only sign laws. On the other side of the debate, (above) a fevered crowd roared in defence of Bill 101 during the language crisis over bilingual signs. (GAZETTE – DAVE SIDAWAY AND PETER ANDREWS)

He styled himself the boy from Baie Comeau, but Brian Mulroney had long been a Montrealer by adoption when he became national leader of the Progressive Conservative party and the first Tory leader since John A. Macdonald to win successive majorities in Parliament. Here he is with wife Mila cheering a goal by the Canadian all stars against the Soviet Union at the Forum in 1987. (GAZETTE – ANDRÉ PICHETTE)

After the stunning Liberal loss to the Parti Québécois in 1976, it was presumed Robert Bourassa's career would be over, after six years in power. In the most remarkable comeback in Canadian political history, he was restored in 1985 and went on to serve eight more years. Accompanied by his wife, Andrée, he cast his ballot for the 1989 election, the last of his career in which he was re-elected by a landslide. Bourassa died in 1996. (GAZETTE – PETER MARTIN)

The most peripatetic of Quebec's leading political figures this century, Lucien Bouchard has been in his time a follower of Maurice Duplessis, Pierre Trudeau and René Lévesque; a member of the Progressive Conservative Party and the Parti Québécois; a federal cabinet minister and a provincial premier; Canada's ambassador to France and the separatist leader of Her Majesty's Loyal Opposition. Here he addresses the founding convention of the Bloc Québécois, the federal sovereignist party he rallied in 1990 before taking over as PQ leader and premier in 1996. He was re-elected in 1998. (GAZETTE – DAVE SIDAWAY)

The prime of "Monsieur" Jacques Parizeau. The PQ premier acknowledges cheers at a Montreal rally during the 1995 referendum on Quebec independence. Parizeau's Yes side would lose by a whisker. His term as premier is memorable mostly for his comments on referendum night: "We (francophones) voted at 60 percent. We were beaten by money and ethnic votes." (GAZETTE – ANDRÉ PICHETTE)

Three days before the 1995 Quebec referendum, federalists turned out in the thousands in downtown Montreal for a unity rally in support of a united Canada. (GAZETTE – ANDRÉ PICHETTE)

St. Jean Baptiste Day parades have changed over the century. The traditional hallmark of the parades for most of the century was a curly-headed boy leading a lamb (above), as in this photo from the 1964 procession. In later years, political overtones replaced the parade's former religious theme, and became an occasion for Quebec sovereignists to vent their nationalist fervour as in the 1995 parade (left), the year of the second sovereignty referendum. For many, the parade has became an occasion for a fun time, as these patriotically painted young ladies (right) seem to be having at the 1998 parade. (MONTREAL STAR AND GAZETTE – JOHN KENNEY AND ANDRÉ PICHETTE)

Mine, mine, all mine. Newly anointed mayor Pierre Bourque exulted on the Mount Royal lookout the morning after he won the 1994 civic election. His re-election in 1998 ensured that he would probably be the century's last mayor of Montreal, and the first of the new millennium. (GAZETTE – DAVE SIDAWAY)

(left) Political foes united in mourning for former premier Robert Bourassa in the fall of 1996. Premier Lucien Bouchard and his wife Audrey (foreground) along with Prime Minister Jean Chrétien and his wife Aline leave Notre Dame Basilica after the funeral. (GAZETTE – JOHN MAHONEY)

On the March

HUBERT **BAUCH**

The last great Montreal parade of the 1900s was a triumph for a movement that at the dawn of the century dared not speak its name, or show its face in polite company. The words shame and embarrassment were then most commonly associated with homosexuality; gay pride would have been an oxymoron in the Victorian context.

But by the century's end, gay pride had gone not only mainstream, but main street with an annual parade that has come to rank as one of the city's most popular street celebrations.

An early Montreal landmark for the women's movement was the 1912 appointment of Carrie Mathilda Derick (seen here in 1890) as a professor of botany at McGill University, making her the first woman ever to be ranked a full professor at a Canadian university. At the time, women were denied the vote and would not get the right federally until 1918. Quebec women, who faced an even greater challenge of discrimination in a province dominated by Catholic paternalism, were granted the right to vote in provincial elections in 1940. (NOTMAN PHOTOGRAPHIC ARCHIVES, MCCORD MUSEUM OF CANADIAN HISTORY, MONTREAL)

PREVIOUS PAGES

An outgrowth of a protest movement against police harassment of homosexual gatherings, Montreal's annual "Divers/Cité" gay pride parade has grown into one of the most popular events on the city's street festival calendar since the first parade in 1993. The 1999 version attracted an estimated 500,000 people, matching the long-entrenched St. Patrick's and St. Jean Baptiste parades. (GAZETTE – PHIL CARPENTER)

The fervour of Quebec's labour movement in its turbulent decades is captured in this 1971 photo of Montreal construction workers rejoicing in a strike vote. (GAZETTE FILES)

The Gazette account of the 1999 version reported glittering drag queens and bare-chested men cavorting atop balloon-lined floats, and dancers on the "Sisters" float flourishing feather boas and pounding tribal drums as the procession wound down venerable St. Joseph Boulevard.

Not so long ago, such a spectacle would more likely have been stoned from the sidewalks than cheered by crowds in the hundreds of thousands, waving rainbow flags and blowing pink whistles. In only its seventh year, the cleverly dubbed Divers/Cité parade drew an estimated 500,000 people, rivaling the best turnouts for the city's historically entrenched St. Jean Baptiste and St. Patrick's Day parades and the biggest of Stanley Cup revels. It has become a celebration not just of homosexual emancipation, but of Montreal's estimation of itself as the city that not only respects difference, but rejoices in diversity.

The gay pride movement is one of many movements that have both reflected and shaped Montreal this century. Some have been more successful than others, and some have been for worse instead of better. But for better or for worse, a vibrant city is by nature alive with movements, and this century, as for all its lifetime, Montreal has been a city of movements. Some have been Montreal-centred movements, at least in their origin: the Quiet Revolution and the Quebec separatist movement; others have been local manifestations of universal movements, notably the women's movement, the labour movement and the radical student movement of the 1960s. Montreal's very founding was inspired by a movement – the 16th century European counter-reformation movement, a backlash against the rise of Protestantism that fostered a competitive missionary colonization of the recently discovered New World. The charter purpose of the Paris syndicate that sponsored Paul de Chomedey de Maisonneuve's 1642 founding expedition to what would

While she was the daughter of one of Montreal's most prominent financiers, Sir Rodolphe Forget, Thérèse Casgrain was also one of the leading lights of Canada's socialist movement. Paying her homage in this 1957 photo are Robert Cliche (left), who would go on to lead the Quebec NDP, and former Saskatchewan premier Tommy Douglas. (MONTREAL STAR – MORRIS EDWARDS)

At the turn of the century, when early feminist Marie Gérin-Lajoie was advocating the need for information on birth control, abortionists and their patients risked life imprisonment and a woman who self-aborted risked seven years in jail. Gérin-Lajoie is best known for her in lobbying for changes to Quebec's Civil Code to recognize rights for married women. (GAZETTE FILES)

Claire Kirkland-Casgrain became the first woman elected to the National Assembly and Quebec's first female cabinet minister, after she was elected in a 1961 by-election in the Montreal riding of Jacques Cartier. Here she wields a pickaxe at the ground-breaking ceremony for the enlargement of LaSalle Catholic High School in 1971. (MONTREAL STAR – BILL ROBSON)

Montrealer Jeanne Sauvé registered another milestone for the women's movement when she was appointed Canada's first female governor-general. Here she inspects her foot guards upon her arrival on Parliament Hill to deliver the Throne Speech at the 1984 opening of Parliament. (GAZETTE – JOHN MAHONEY)

become Montreal was "the conversion of the savages" in the far reaches of New France.

Montreal itself was in movement from the outset of the 20th century, both upward and outward. The city's mid-town moved progressively uptown during the century's first two decades, from the Old Montreal streets that had been the city's hub since the days of Dollier de Casson. Such lordly Montreal houses of retail as Morgan's, Ogilvy's and Birks relocated up Beaver Hall Hill, making Ste. Catherine Street the city's commercial locus, a distinction it has retained through ups and downs ever since. (The late and venerable Dupuis Frères was there from the start.) St. Laurent Boulevard was widened up from what was then Craig Street (now St. Antoine) and The Main came into being as the dividing line between East and

West in Montreal, as well as the city's wickedest and most wondrous thoroughfare. During the same period, Montreal was also spreading as one of the great North American movements of the century took hold in Montreal – the migration to suburbia. The Town of Mount Royal is an example of one of the continent's first planned suburbs and the visionary product of a corporate marriage of railway and real estate interests, laid out with all its main streets radiating from the commuter train station.

Montreal's cosmopolitan stew of ethnicities and classes makes it a natural breeding ground for social and political movements. Among the movements that have come farthest this century in Montreal are the women's movement and the labour movement, both of which were in relative infancy at the turn of the century, and considered equally subversive in the right-thinking mainstream of the day.

Women had already established themselves as a vital pillar of the national workforce by 1900, though a disproportionate number toiled in sweatshops and what would become known in more militant times as gender ghetto jobs, and farm women were considered to have no occupation. One in six Canadian workers was a woman; a quarter of the manufacturing and mechanical jobs in the country were held by women; three-quarters of the nation's teachers were women. And yet women were denied the vote in Canadian elections until 1918. Quebec women faced an even greater challenge of discrimination in a province that for the first half of the century was dominated by a paternalistic Roman Catholic church hierarchy that held women to be lesser beings than men. While other provinces followed the federal suit in 1922, Quebec women were not granted the vote in provincial elections until 1940. It helped that Montreal's most influential early feminists came from some of the city's leading gentry. Marie Gérin-Lajoie, the mother of Quebec's women's movement, was from a family of blue-chip jurists; the most famous of all Quebec feminists was Thérèse Casgrain, daughter of Sir Rodolphe Forget, one of the foremost of Montreal's 19th-century financiers. Montreal landmarks on the long road to women's liberation include the appointment of Carrie Mathilda Derick as a professor of botany at McGill, the first female named a full professor at a Canadian university; a minimum wage law for women in 1935; an all-women symphony orchestra formed in 1940, which lasted 20 years and became the first Canadian orchestra to play Carnegie Hall; the first woman to become governor-general was Montrealer Jeanne Sauvé, who was also the first woman to serve as speaker of the House of Commons. It was Montreal

Montreal obstetrician Henry Morgentaler became a hero of the Canadian feminist movement with his crusade to liberalize Canada's abortion laws by openly performing abortions at his Montreal clinic. In November 1973, Morgentaler won the first of three acquittals on charges of performing illegal abortions. Clinical abortions were legitimized when provincial authorities conceded that no jury could be found to convict him. (GAZETTE – LEN SIDAWAY)

Women were a force in the Parti Québécois from its earliest days. Gathered here at a Montreal press conference are some of the party's women candidates in the 1976 provincial election, some of whom went on to sit in the National Assembly and hold prominent cabinet posts. From left, Hélène Savard-Jacob, Denise Leblanc, Line Bourgeois, Lise Payette, Louise Beaudoin and Louise Cuerrier-Sauvé. (GAZETTE FILES)

Before entering politics, René Lévesque made a name for himself as a broadcaster and union activist in the years following the Asbestos strike. In this 1959 photo, a bemused-looking Lévesque stands between policemen at the doors of the downtown station where he was detained after being arrested at a demonstration in support of 74 striking Radio-Canada producers. (GAZETTE FILES)

The Quebec labour movement really came into its own in the '60s under the inspired leadership of Jean Marchand (pictured above, right, in 1965 with Jacques Hébert and Jean-Louis Roux), who had led the Asbestos strikers in the late1940s, and Gérard Picard, (top) a former Quebec NDP leader who went on to build the Confederation of National Trade Unions into the province's first independent labour federation. (Gazette files)

The "Common Front" strike by provincial public employees in 1972 set the tone for labour relations for years to come when Quebec's major labour federations united to wrest a new "social contract" from the government. In the 1970s, the labour movement believed that gains won for public sector workers would have a locomotive effect on working conditions in private inductry. Here, marching arm-in-arm on centre stage, are the Common Front leaders who were jailed for defying a back-to-work law in 1972. From left: Yvon Charbonneau of the Quebec teachers federation, Louis Laberge of the Quebec Federation of Labour (in light-coloured suit), and Marcel Pépin of the Confederation of National Trade Unions. (MONTREAL STAR – GEORGE BIRD)

doctor Henry Morgentaler who frontally challenged the country's abortion law, which denied women control of their own bodies. One of the most dramatic and decisive Montreal political events of the century was the "Yvettes" women's rally during the 1980 Quebec sovereignty referendum. The more than 10,000 women who filled the Forum in support of the federalist No side constituted the largest gathering of women in the province's history which is widely credited with turning the referendum

tide in favour of a united Canada. As the century ended, the Quebec cabinet had a higher ratio of women than any other in the country.

In the annals of Quebec's labour movement, the century's most storied strike was the 1949 workers' uprising in Asbestos, when the miners stood their ground against the authority of the almighty Duplessis regime and its provincial police enforcers. But Montreal has been Quebec's union central throughout the century, home to most of the province's unionized workers and the headquarters of the major provincial labour organizations; the historical figures associated with the Asbestos strike – Jean Marchand, the strike leader; Pierre Trudeau, its intellectual agitator; and Jean Drapeau, its legal counsel – were all commuters from Montreal.

At the dawn of the 20th century, Montreal captains of industry were still smarting from the fairly recent imposition of child labour laws, and in the board-of-trade purview, unions were party to a Bolshevik conspiracy, an association that some of the labour rhetoric of the day and the brandishing of red flags at union rallies tended to invite. Montreal at the time was the country's dominant railway town, and it was a signal triumph for the local labour movement when CPR workers won the right to be represented by the trainmen's brotherhood after an 11-week strike in 1901. Montreal police and fire fighters got union recognition in 1943, the day after a December strike vote; a one-day police strike in 1969 invited the wildest night of rioting in Montreal history. It would take more than a half century after the trainmen's strike for the Quebec labour movement to come fully into its own under the inspired leadership of Marchand and Gérard Picard, who built the Confederation of National Trade Unions into the province's first independent labour and led the struggle to unionize key industries and gain collective bargaining rights for public servants.

A pioneering figure in both the women's movement and the labour movement in the 1930s and 1940s was union leader and activist Lea Roback, who headed the union at RCA Victor, one of the city's major employers, and led the fight against sexual abuse of female workers by employers. Madeleine Parent was also prominent in the struggle for the rights of workers and women.

The measure of the labour movement's success this century is that the province today

Lea Roback, a prominent Montreal pioneer of both the labour movement and the women's movement in the first half of the century. (GAZETTE FILES)

has the most stringent labour laws in the country and the highest percentages of unionized workers.

Montreal movements have come from left, right and centre this century. The spectrum ranges from Anaclet Chalifoux, the brown-shirted Montreal *führer* of the Fascist Party of Canada, which claimed 25,000 adherents in the 1930s, to "Red" Fred Rose, the local commissar of the Labour Progressive Party, who was elected to Parliament in a midtown Montreal riding the following decade, despite his Marxist persuasions and Stalinist sympathies. Rose fell victim to the postwar commie witchhunt movement in 1946,

The 1970s were violent years on Montreal's labour front, especially during conflicts in which management brought in strikebreakers to replace striking workers. This photo of a strikebreaker guarding the Robin Hood Multifoods plant in Montreal during a 1977 strike is a classic. During the conflict, guards opened fire on strikers, wounding eight people. The incident was one of many that prompted the PQ government to bring in anti-strikebreaker legislation – the first in Canada – which was credited with reducing picket-line violence. (GAZETTE – TEDD CHURCH)

A rash of fascist organizations sprang up in Montreal during the 1930s, echoing the rise of Mussolini, Hitler and Franco in Europe. Here, members of the ladies' auxiliary connected to the Parti National Socialiste Chrétien proudly sport their swastika blouses in a photo taken in 1938. (GAZETTE FILES)

when he was sentenced to six years in prison for passing wartime secrets to the Soviet Union, notwithstanding that the Soviets were Canada's wartime ally. In between were the movements for social democracy and civil rights, whose Montreal champions include lawyer, professor and poet Frank Scott, who defended the right of Jehovah's Witnesses to propagate their faith in the province, and his McGill University law faculty colleague John Peters Humphrey, the principal author of the Universal Declaration of Human Rights, hailed upon its recent 50th anniversary as the Magna Carta of all humanity.

Perhaps the most sweeping Quebec movement of the century, which in keeping with Quebec movements spread from Montreal, has been the progressive secularization of what was once commonly – and all too validly – known as the "priest-ridden province." Four Quebecers out of five still profess to be Catholic, but fewer than one in four qualify as practicing Catholics;

Catholics; from being the most diligent church-going population in the country, Quebecers have gone to being the least actively devotional in the years since the Quiet Revolution. And yet, it was a church movement – the Catholic Action lay movement, whose national headquarters was in Montreal – that produced some of the leading political lights of Quebec's modern age, including Marc Lalonde, Claude Ryan, Jeanne Sauvé and Gérard Pelletier. In the words of their contemporary, the eminent Montreal sociologist Guy Rocher, they established the beachhead of the Quiet Revolution, which in a sense was a confluence of all Montreal movements of the century.

The Quebec nationalist movement has taken all three paths this century, moving from right to left to centre in the course of its evolution. It was decidedly right-wing in its early-century incarnation, when its seminal inspiration was Abbé Lionel Groulx, who blended

Restaurant owner Frank Roncarelli, a leader of Quebec's Jehovah's Witnesses movement, was at the centre of a celebrated civil liberties case in the 1940s. He launched a landmark court challenge against the Duplessis government when it tried to stifle his religious activism by taking away the liquor license for his Crescent Street café. His lawyer was Frank Scott, who was a pillar of the McGill law faculty in his day job. (GAZETTE FILES)

Montreal's most famous communist of the century was Fred Rose, shown with his wife in a 1940s photo, who was elected to Parliament in 1944. Rose was sentenced two years later to six years in prison for passing wartime secrets to the Soviet Union. The key witness against him was Soviet defector Igor Gouzenko, who first alerted North Americans to the Soviet Union's Cold War espionage network. (GAZETTE FILES)

The United Nations Universal Declaration of Human Rights has been called humanity's Magna Carta. Its principal author was McGill University law professor John P. Humphrey, pictured here in 1983. (GAZETTE – TEDD CHURCH)

old-time Catholic religion with fascist political ideology in a potent appeal to the "French-Canadian race."

With its turn toward separatism in the 1960s, Quebec nationalism also made a quantum ideological lurch from the neo-Nazi right to the Aquarian New Left, from national socialism to social democracy. Its extremist element, the Front de Libération du Québec, drew its inspiration from the mid-century colonial liberation movements in the third world and their attendant urban guerrilla factions. The public revulsion against the campaign of FLQ terrorism culminating in the 1970 October Crisis, and the discipline of power after the Parti

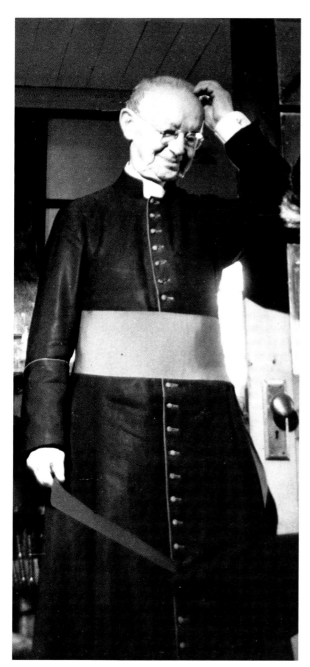

Abbé Lionel Groulx is commonly hailed as a hero of modern Quebec nationalism, despite his prominent fascist and anti-Semitic propensities. He is shown here in 1959 during the filming of a documentary on his life. (GAZETTE FILES - MONTREAL STAR)

The French-first language movement that arose in the mid-1960s culminated a decade later in Bill 101, the Parti Québécois language law. This 1969 protest is against the first provincial language law, Bill 63, which infuriated Quebec nationalists by granting English equal status with French. (Gazette – Aussie Whiting)

A firebomb lights up the night as militant separatists taunt riot police during a 1969 demonstration outside the old Montreal courthouse on Notre Dame Street. (GAZETTE FILES)

Québécois became the provincial government six years later, steered the sovereignist movement to its present centrist course where, under Lucien Bouchard, it is social democratic in pretension and conservative in practice, and in sum, quintessentially Canadian. Since the rise of the separatist movement, Montreal has been the barometer of its fortunes. It was Montreal that gave the PQ its first block of seats in the National Assembly in the early 1970s, but it was the preponderance of federalist support in Montreal in both the 1980 and 1995 referendums that carried the day for Canada.

Coincident with the waning of support for sovereignty since the last referendum was the rise of the partitionist movement, which also sprang from Montreal and southwestern Quebec, and which envisaged a breakaway from a secessionist Quebec.

From its beginnings, Montreal has been both the sum of its people and the product of its people. Movements have come and gone, and new ones will arise in the century to come. For better or for worse, Montreal has gone where its movements have taken it. ◆

T-shirts lionizing convicted FLQ murderer Paul Rose were a fashion note at this 1971 protest against the War Measures Act. (MONTREAL STAR – PAUL TAILLEFER)

Peace and love and rock & roll. Former Beatle John Lennon and new bride Yoko Ono stretched out in a Queen Elizabeth Hotel suite during their 1968 "bed-in" for peace. During their stay, Lennon recorded the flower-power anthem, Give Peace a Chance. All together now: "All we are sayyying … " (GAZETTE – TEDD CHURCH)

No, not a ticker-tape parade. The radical students movement of the late 1960s achieved its Montreal apotheosis – or its nadir, depending on one's point of view – during the February 1969 occupation of the computer centre in the Hall Building of what was then Sir George Williams University (now Concordia). Students set the upper-storey computer centre on fire in a final rampage. The rioting students also blanketed Mackay Street with computer filing cards and teletype paper tossed from the windows. Ninety-seven students were arrested when police moved in, and damage was estimated at nearly $2 million. (GAZETTE FILES)

The native rights movement turned violent with a fury in the summer of 1990. In this photo from the first day of the so-called Oka Crisis, a masked member of the Mohawk Warrior Society brandishes his rifle defiantly atop an overturned Sûreté du Québec patrol car on the Oka road barricaded for more than a month by armed native activists, who also blocked the Mercier Bridge for much of the summer. (GAZETTE – JOHN KENNEY)

Entrepreneurs:
the spirit that
moves our country.

Money Makers

JAY **BRYAN**

A S THE LAST DAYS OF 1899 trickled away, celebration of the new century was muted among Montreal's business leaders. The Gazette's financial page noted that the Bank of England had just hiked its discount rate to "the extremely high figure of 6 per cent" as it sought to finance the Boer War in South Africa, and this was no good for the stock market. Turning to the shipping page, one found more grumbling. During the just-ended navigation season, "rates were not quite what steamship men desired," and the volume

Canada's first transcontinental transport giant, the Canadian Pacific Railway Co., was one of several companies that symbolized Montreal's central position in the Canadian economy when the century began. This Canadian Pacific photo was taken in 1900 at the Beaconsfield station. CPR's Angus Works, the largest railway shops in the world at the turn of the century, made Montreal the transportation hub of Canada. By the end of the century, the parent company, Canadian Pacific Ltd., had moved its operations to Calgary. (GAZETTE FILES)

PREVIOUS PAGES

At the turn of the century, St. James Street's Bank of Montreal building, the Royal Bank building (shown here) and others were shrines to the immense wealth and power in the hands of Montrealers of British descent. By the 1920s, as the America's industrial heartland gained strength, the westward shift of Canada's economic centre had begun. Montreal's importance slowly began to wane. (GAZETTE - GORDON BECK)

Bombardier, one of the most dramatic business success stories of the century, was begun by Joseph-Armand Bombardier in the small town of Valcourt. Bombardier invented the snowmobile and developed several models including this one in 1942 for the Canadian Army. (GAZETTE FILES)

of shipping had diminished, "several of the largest vessels . . . having been taken up by the Imperial Government as transports for the South African war."

But these were temporary annoyances. The wealthy financial, shipping, railway and manufacturing magnates of Montreal could bask in the knowledge that they absolutely dominated Canada's economy. In some cases, their interests stretched around the globe. They drew their power from close trading and financial ties to Britain, the financial centre of the world. The richest of them all was Donald Smith, whose Bank of Montreal – the biggest bank in Canada – had financial and management ties to a mighty group of companies that included the country's first transcontinental transport giant, the

St. James Street, now officially St. Jacques, was the bustling heart of commerce in Montreal at the beginning of the 20th century as this 1910 street scene attests. But in the following decades, major retailers moved up the hill to open shop on Ste. Catherine Street, as did the venerable old Montreal house of Morgan's (now The Bay) whose emporium still stands on Phillips Square. (GAZETTE FILES)

In 1912, Montreal opened the largest concrete grain elevator in the world at the time. City officials said it was just in the nick of time – the amount of grain going through the port had increased 26-fold in the previous five years. (GAZETTE FILES)

Canadian Pacific Railway; most important telecommunications firm, Bell Telephone; and later on the biggest domestic shipper, Canada Steamship Lines; dominant insurer, Sun Life Assurance Co., and leading textile maker, Dominion Textile.

Already in 1899, Montreal's major firms were giants on a global scale. The CPR, whose Angus Works in Montreal were the largest railway shops in the world, brought in wheat and other commodities from all over Canada. This position as Canada's transport hub nourished many other enterprises, including Ogilvie Mills, which became the biggest flour company in the world. By the turn of the century, Sun Life was already active in the Caribbean, Latin America and China, and well on its way to becoming the biggest insurer in Canada. As the 1920s ended, it had a staff of 1,500 headquar-

tered in the largest office structure in the British Empire, Montreal's Sun Life Building.

Historian Robert Sweeny has unearthed Sun Life's instructions to an executive being sent to prospect the Middle East and Africa in 1891, making it clear that the concept of a global economy was already a reality for some companies: "When your work in the Eastern Mediterranean is finished, strike down the Red Sea for the east coast of Africa. . . . You can if you think well of it run over to Madagascar. You should certainly take in Mauritius. After leaving Cape Colony, take coasting steamers, again stopping at every little settlement on the west coast, but don't go up the Congo. In this way you will in time reach Senegal."

It was an era of industrial consolidation, with Canada's economic power concentrated in the hands of just a few enormously powerful Montreal financiers and industrialists. Nearly all were English-speaking, but as McGill University economic historian Mary MacKinnon has noted, religion could be as important a key to economic success as language. Those who benefited from all-important British business connections were Protestants. Jewish businessmen and Catholics, whether French-Canadian or Irish, might be notably successful within Quebec, but couldn't easily break into the Imperial business circle. Thus the one Irish member of Montreal's business elite early in the century was Herbert Holt, a Protestant.

Not long after the turn of the century, Holt, who began his career as an engineer designing sections of the CPR line, picked up Donald Smith's mantle as the most powerful tycoon in town. He came to control about 300 companies on three continents that produced, among other things, 10 per cent of the world's newsprint supply, recounts Peter Newman, chronicler of Canada's business establishment. Holt's key position was president of the Royal

The Gazette is Montreal's oldest newspaper, founded in 1778, and its sole remaining English paper. But many other English news-papers have thrived in Montreal. The Montreal Star was the largest English newspaper for most of this century but it closed for good in 1979. The Gazette acquired its buildings and photo archives in 1980. (GAZETTE FILES - MONTREAL STAR)

Bank of Canada, from which he exercised influence over a group of satellite companies. (The Royal Bank had migrated to Montreal from Halifax in 1907, following the lead of the Bank of Nova Scotia. Both would later move their key executives to Toronto.)

The Holt interests came to include Montreal Trust, Famous Players Corp., Consolidated Paper and Montreal Light, Heat and Power Co., which was for a time the world's largest privately owned utility. Montreal Light, Heat and Power was also an enormously profitable monopoly, helping to explain a deep current of public animosity toward Holt. When he died in 1941, a baseball game at De Lorimier Stadium was interrupted so his death could be announced. William Weintraub describes the crowd's reaction in City Unique, his history of Montreal in the 1940s and '50s: "There was a moment of

stunned silence, and then a prolonged outburst of cheers and applause."

Contrary to the popular image of the franco-phone community as having little interest in commercial activities before the coming of the Quiet Revolution, it actually produced several generations of talented bankers and industrialists. Early in the century, a leading example was Louis-Joseph Forget, a former president of the Montreal Stock Exchange and powerful financier who would work with Herbert Holt to merge several utility companies into the giant Montreal Light, Heat and Power Co. In the 1920s, Senator Frédéric-Liguori Béique was president of the Banque Canadienne Nationale (a predecessor of today's Banque Nationale du Canada) and a member of the CPR's executive committee. In the Saguenay region, J.E.A. Dubuc built up the Compagnie de Pulpe de

Chicoutimi, constructed the harbor at Port-Alfred and exported pulp to England. In Sorel, Joseph Simard put together a diversified industrial empire.

Jewish businesses, like francophone ones, couldn't count on a helping hand from British capital, but this didn't prevent the Bronfman brothers, Sam, Harry, Abe and Allan, from founding not one, but two great business empires. Sam's branch of the family built Montreal-based Seagram Co. into the world's biggest liquor company and, more recently, a powerful presence in the U.S. entertainment business, with its headquarters now in New York City. Allan's sons, Peter and Edward, created Toronto's Edper Group, a conglomerate that at one point employed 60,000 workers and had interests in finance, resources, electric power and real estate.

Seagram, the larger of the Bronfman empires and the one that remains in family hands, reflected the shift in Canada's economy toward closer links with the U.S. Along with this link came a gradual shift westward in Canada's centre of economic gravity. By the 1920s, Britain "was beginning to look a little tired" as a world financial centre, suggests McGill University his-

There were many powerful and wealthy men in Montreal but few were as powerful as Herbert Holt, an Irish Protestant(top). Holt's interests came to include Montreal Trust, Famous Players Corp., Consolidated Paper and Montreal Light, Heat and Power Co., which was once the world's largest privately owned utility. (Gazette files – The Standard)

Financier Max Aitken, who later became Lord Beaverbrook, founded the Steel Co. of Canada (Stelco) in Montreal in 1910. He is seen here with his son. (Gazette files)

Jewish businesses, like francophone ones, couldn't count on a helping hand in English business circles. But that didn't prevent Sam Bronfman's family from building Montreal-based Seagram Co. into the world's biggest liquor company and, more recently, a powerful presence in the U.S. entertainment business. Both of Sam's sons, Edgar and Charles (shown in bottom photo when they were children in the late 1930s), have left Montreal to settle in New York. (Gazette files)

torian Brian Young, while the massive U.S. economy was coming into its prime. The most important U.S. industry, automobiles, was concentrated right across the border from Ontario. U.S. automakers soon had several plants in the rich industrial and agricultural market stretching between Toronto and Windsor. Toronto, which had the good fortune to be "right on the doorstep of the U.S. industrial heartland," in the words of Concordia University historian Graeme Decarie, became a key conduit for U.S. flows of capital into Canada and an increasingly powerful centre of industry and finance. Montreal's importance slowly, almost imperceptibly, began to wane.

Of course, the position of Montreal was greatly worsened by self-inflicted wounds. There was the complacency of Montreal's old anglo business elite, reflected in such lost opportunities as the reluctance of the blue-chip Montreal Stock Exchange to deal in the more speculative share issues that helped to finance Canada's nascent mining industry in the 1920s. By the mid-1930s, the Toronto Stock Exchange, which had been happy to profit from the new interest in mining exploration, surpassed its Montreal rival and accounted for a majority of stock trading in Canada. There was the cost of failed government policies, like the disastrous decision in the 1970s to force international flights into the cost-

By the end of the century, Bombardier had grown into a major international powerhouse in everything from jet aircraft to mass-transit equipment under the leadership of Bombardier's son-in-law, Laurent Beaudoin, (top) shown in this 1998 photo. (GAZETTE - PHIL CARPENTER)

Pierre Péladeau built Quebecor, which publishes Le Journal de Montréal and several other newspapers and magazines, into a financial and international communications giant. His sons, Pierre-Karl and Érik, stepped into their fathers' shoes after his death in 1997. (GAZETTE - LEN SIDAWAY)

From humble beginnings, Jean Coutu (bottom) built an international drugstore empire. (GAZETTE - LEN SIDAWAY).

By the mid-1930s, Montreal's stock exchange had been surpassed by its Toronto rival which accounted for a majority of stock trading in Canada. By the end of the century, its position had been further weakened. The 125-year-old Montreal Exchange announced that its traders, like those in this 1999 photo, would concentrate on futures and options trading only. (GAZETTE - JOHN KENNEY)

ly new Mirabel airport. This made it impossible for Dorval to perform its function as Canada's key airline "hub" where passengers from international flights could transfer conveniently to domestic ones and vice versa, points out urbanologist Mario Polèse of the Institut National de la Recherche Scientifique. The result was that Toronto replaced Montreal in this role, a loss that is unlikely ever to be reversed.

The most dramatic change, of course, was the rise of Quebec nationalism and the coming to power of a Parti Québécois government in 1976. Members of the business establishment, still mostly anglophone, had been forced to come to terms with big changes in Quebec since the Quiet Revolution began more than a decade earlier, but the election of an avowedly separatist government and the imposition of

The most dramatic change in Montreal's business climate came with the rise of Quebec nationalism – the Quiet Revolution of the 1960s and the election of the pro-independence Parti Québécois government in 1976. René Lévesque was the mastermind behind the Lesage government's plan to expropriate private power companies and create the Hydro-Québec monopoly. Lévesque, shown in this 1963 photo with a model hydro tower, abandoned the Liberals in 1968. (MONTREAL STAR – PAUL GÉLINAS)

sweeping language laws constituted an unprecedented shock. Within two years of that election, Reed Scowen, a Liberal member of the National Assembly, had compiled a list of 43 companies that had moved either their headquarters or a significant part of their operations out of Quebec. Nearly all had been based in Montreal.

Scowen estimated that these moves resulted in the loss of more than 5,500 jobs. Even more serious than the job loss was the final destruction of Montreal's already faltering position as a Canada's leading head-office city. One by one, the remaining business giants moved their headquarters operations out of town. Among them were several of Canada's most important financial companies: Sun Life, Royal Bank of Canada, Bank of Montreal and Royal

Trust. Montreal also lost the headquarters of the country's two leading high-tech companies, Northern Telecom and CAE Industries. Finally, just after Quebec's second referendum on secession, came the crowning blow. Canadian Pacific announced in November of 1995 that the headquarters of its transcontinental rail system – a network that once symbolized Montreal's central position in the Canadian economy – would move to Calgary. Within another two years, the parent company, Canadian Pacific Ltd., was also in Calgary.

But for all its travails, Montreal was far from finished. If it could no longer be the command centre of Canadian business, it would seek to be a centre of the emerging knowledge economy. Its plants and research centres still turn out some of the most advanced telecommunications technologies, aerospace equipment and pharmaceutical products to be found anywhere. The city's deep roots in these industries go all the way back to the turn of the century, when telecommunications pioneer Bell Canada (now Bell Canada Enterprises) was already an important corporate presence and drug laboratories like those of Wyeth (now Wyeth-Ayerst Canada), Frosst (now Merck Frosst Canada) and Rougier were being established. The aerospace industry can trace its history back to the aircraft division of Canadian Vickers in the 1920s, an establishment that would pass through several owners, eventually becoming today's Canadair division of Bombardier, a successful maker of business jets and small airliners.

And parallel with the rise of nationalism that made the traditional anglo business elite so uncomfortable came a new wave of entrepreneurs who owed nothing to the old establishment. Some of them would create great new dynasties. As the century drew to a close, perhaps the most dramatic success story was that of Bombardier Inc., the very archetype of a Quebec company. Based on the development of the snowmobile by mechanic Joseph-Armand Bombardier in the small town of Valcourt, it grew into a major international presence in everything from jet aircraft to mass-transit equipment under the leadership of Bombardier's son-in-law and successor, Laurent Beaudoin. Other family business empires include Paul Desmarais's Power Corp, a financial and communications giant; Pierre Péladeau's Quebecor, a communications and printing powerhouse; the international drugstore empire of Jean Coutu; and André Chagnon's Groupe Vidéotron, with its sprawling cable-television interests.

Appropriately for a high-tech city, some of Montreal's most important new success stories are in advanced technologies. Under Charles Sirois, Teleglobe Inc. has become one of the most aggressive and fast-growing telecommunications companies in Canada. Scientist Francesco Bellini has built Biochem Pharma into Canada's most successful biotechnology company, producer of the world's leading treatment for AIDS. Lorne Trottier and partner Branko Matic have turned their company, Matrox, into one of the world's biggest makers of computer-graphics equipment. And there's another source of strength: what consulting economist Marcel Côté calls the Céline Dion phenomenon. Côté is referring to the ability of creative Quebecers to develop their talent within the protective cocoon of a francophone culture that insulates them somewhat from North American competitive forces. Every so often, someone of outstanding talent bursts forth from this cocoon to conquer the rest of the world. Apart from Dion, the pop-music phenomenon of her generation, examples include the Cirque du Soleil and the Cossette advertising and marketing empire.

Creativity, of course, includes everything from mass entertainment to industrial research, which is what ties an outfit like the Cirque du Soleil to a seemingly very different one like Biochem Pharma. In Côté's view, such creativity could spark an era of renewed growth in Montreal. The struggle for dominance as Canada's trading, deal-making and headquarters city is over. Toronto has won. But Côté sees every chance that Montreal will find a satisfying new vocation, prospering from the creative sparks given off by its unique blend of cultures and the ability to hold on to homegrown entrepreneurs, who know they can't find another city like this anywhere in North America. ◆

The world famous Cirque du Soleil (right), which has dazzled audiences world-wide with contortions and costumes like those in this photo, was begun by Guy Laliberté and Daniel Gauthier. (GAZETTE - DAVE SIDAWAY)

Playing to win

RED **FISHER**

F OR MANY MONTREALERS, hockey always has been more than just a game. It is our hopes, dreams, our culture and even our national identity. Montreal fans always have had a special feeling for their professional sports heroes, but no athlete has meant as much to them as Maurice Richard. He still does. Richard represented something good to everyone, which is why hockey fans were in a foul mood on March 17, 1955.

The city was a firecracker waiting to explode because the "Rocket" had been sus-

Maurice Richard was the best – and fiercest – of Montreal's hockey favourites. (GAZETTE FILES)

pended by NHL president Clarence Campbell for the last three games of the regular season and the entire playoffs in the wake of an ugly stick-swinging incident. The Detroit Red Wings were in the city, but the Canadiens would be playing without their icon.

Richard had been the best – and fiercest – of hockey's superstars for a decade. Every opponent wanted a piece of him, and he of them, from the moment he became the first player to score 50 goals in a 50-game season in 1945. By 1955, 10 years later, the regular-season schedule had increased to 70 games and while Richard no longer was the goal-scorer he had been, his dedication to winning had remained constant. The fire in him still burned.

NHL president Clarence Campbell was mobbed at the Montreal Forum March 17, 1955, by hockey fans angered by the suspension of Canadiens star "Rocket" Richard. Campbell was pelted with eggs and assaulted. Richard had been suspended because of an ugly stick-swinging incident in an earlier game. Rioting broke out during the March 17 game and spread to downtown streets, where angry fans smashed windows and clashed with police. (GAZETTE FILES)

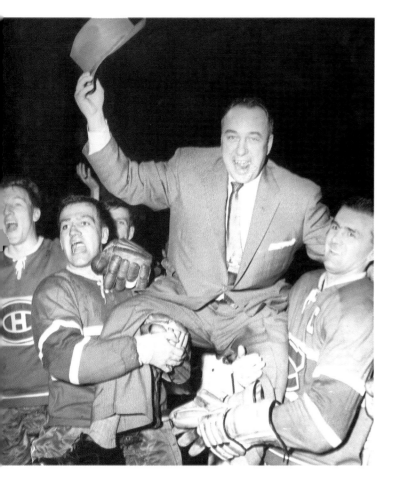

Coach Hector "Toe" Blake (GAZETTE – MONTREAL STAR)

"Boom Boom" Geoffrion, Toe Blake and "Rocket" Richard celebrating 1957 Stanley Cup win. (GAZETTE – MONTREAL STAR)

The stick-swinging had happened in Boston, where Bruins defenceman Hal Laycoe had struck Richard on the side of the head. Richard responded by high-sticking Laycoe on the shoulder and face. Then, when Richard's stick was taken from him, he grabbed another and hit Laycoe twice on the back. Linesman Cliff Thompson, who was trying to restrain Richard, was struck in the face.

Three days later and the day before this Canadiens-Red Wings game in Montreal, Campbell brought down the decision that shook the hockey establishment in general and Montreal fans in particular. Mayor Jean Drapeau had urged Campbell not to attend the St. Patrick's Day game. The NHL's president's response was to arrive at his Forum seat several rows above ice level halfway through the first period. By that time, the Wings led, 2-0. The

moment Campbell was spotted, there were angry cries and threats from groups of fans. Eggs and tomatoes were thrown at the president, who sat in his seat staring straight ahead, trying hard not to pay attention to the furor his appearance had created.

At period's end, a fan walked up several steps toward Campbell, offering to shake hands with the president. Then, when Campbell reached for the outstretched hand, the fan slapped his face. Seconds later, a tear gas bomb exploded. The thick, yellow mass of smoke sent fans screaming toward the main lobby. People were choking, coughing and retching, their eyes streaming. Many yelled "fire!" The building was ordered cleared, and with the Canadiens trailing the Red Wings, 4-1, the decision was made to forfeit the game to the visitors.

Maurice "Rocket" Richard, Dickie Moore and Henri "Pocket Rocket" Richard in 1958. (GAZETTE FILES)

Even today, more than four decades later, people remain bitter over the suspension, which quickly developed into hockey's worst case of violence off the ice. In a matter of minutes, there was an outpouring of looting and burning. Cars were overturned. A mob of thousands shattered windows along Ste. Catherine Street, eventually leading to the arrest of 37 adults and four juveniles. The wonder of it, though, was that nobody was killed on that black night which was to become known as the Richard Riot. The next day, a visibly shaken Richard sat behind a forest of microphones, pleading with the people, his people, to exercise calm.

The Canadiens have been blessed with a flood of superstars en route to an NHL record 24 Stanley Cups: Georges Vézina, Newsy Lalonde, Howie Morenz, Aurèle Joliat, Jean Béliveau, Guy Lafleur, Henri Richard, Doug Harvey, Jacques Plante, Larry Robinson, Dickie Moore, Yvan Cournoyer, Ken Dryden, Bernie Geoffrion and Patrick Roy. The list goes on and on, but there was only one Rocket.

Everything about Richard had little to do with the number of goals he scored: it was the way he scored them. From the blueline in, there was nobody as fierce or as intense. It was the menace implicit within him each time he swooped in on an opposing goaltender. It was in the strength of his arms and in the barrel of his chest which threatened to burst out of his sweater at any moment. It was in the tight line of his mouth, and in the snarl it formed when he was challenged. He was one of a kind in a

The original Forum at the corner of Atwater Avenue and Ste. Catherine Street, built in 1924 for the Montreal Maroons expansion hockey team, held 9,500 seats. This photo was taken just after it was built. (GAZETTE FILES)

Hockey great Aurèle Joliat and Wildor Larochelle pose in 1931. (GAZETTE FILES)

Canadiens star Howie Morenz, lovingly know as the Stratford Streak, dazzled Montreal hockey fans for more than a decade in the '20s and '30s. (GAZETTE FILES - MONTREAL STAR)

The famous Punch Line of the 1940s starred Maurice Richard, Elmer Lach and "Toe" Blake. In 1945, when this photo was shot, helmets were unheard of in hockey. (MONTREAL STANDARD - LOUIS JACQUES)

The Canadiens produced many hockey greats: Howie Morenz, "Rocket" Richard, Guy Lafleur and others. But no one revolutionized the game as did Jacques Plante when he donned a protective mask. In this 1959 photo, Plante's nose was still bandaged from an Andy Bathgate shot when he struck this theatrical pose to show off his new goaler's mask. (GAZETTE FILES)

Jean Béliveau and the Stanley Cup in 1971. In his 18 years with the Canadiens, the team won the cup 10 times. (GAZETTE FILES – MONTREAL STAR)

No hockey series has electrified Canadians like the
Russia-Canada series in
1972. Canada lost the first
game in Montreal 7-3 but
went on to win the series,
after Paul Hendersen scored
the winning goal of the
eighth game. In this photo,
Prime Minister Trudeau
greets the team captains
before the first game at the
Forum. (GAZETTE FILES)

Valery Kharlamov scores on
Team Canada goalie Ken
Dryden after wheeling
around the fallen Don
Awrey. Kharlamov scored
twice in Russia's 7-3 win
over the home team in that
game. (MONTREAL STAR –
ALLAN LEISHMAN)

Pete Mahovlich and Yvan Cournoyer exchange congratulations with Vladislav Tretiak of the Central Red Army of Moscow team after the big New Year's eve game in 1975. (GAZETTE FILES)

Guy Lafleur's "flower power" dazzled on the ice and with Montreal hockey fans. Lafleur and other Canadiens greats were honoured in March 1996 when this photo was taken. (GAZETTE – JOHN MAHONEY)

Maurice "Rocket" Richard and Céline Dion embrace after she performed at the Molson Centre in 1998. Dion, wearing a Habs sweater with Richard's No. 9, delighted the full house with a song dedicated to him. (GAZETTE – JOHN KENNEY)

In May of 1946, Jackie Robinson made history when he joined the Montreal Royals, a farm team for the Brooklyn Dodgers, and became the first black to play professional league baseball. The next year, he was signed by Branch Rickey to play for the Dodgers. His new contract was worth $14,000, twice his Montreal salary. (GAZETTE FILES)

city which has always revered its best athletes. And there have been many in this century.

When Brooklyn Dodgers general manager Branch Rickey struck down major league baseball's colour bar and shipped Jackie Robinson to the International League's Montreal Royals in 1946, Robinson immediately became family. Almost from the moment the Expos drafted their 30 original National League players on October 14, 1968, they became *Nos amours*. Sam Etcheverry and Hal Patterson represented Alouettes football at its best, and for years professional wrestler Yvon Robert attracted fans in sellout numbers to the Forum.

Long before April 14, 1969, when the Expos rallied to defeat the visiting St. Louis Cardinals 8-7 at Jarry Park in the first regular-season major league game ever played outside the United States, the city had the Royals, a Triple-A farm team of the Brooklyn Dodgers, whose home was at De Lorimier Stadium in east-end Montreal. It's where Robinson electrified the crowds in 1945, it's where others such as Roy Campanella and Duke Snider excelled before going to the parent Dodgers.

The Expos had been granted a major league franchise on May 27, 1968, and in hardly any time at all, Montrealers embraced Mack Jones, Coco Laboy, John Boccabella and Manny Mota when they were among "The Original 30" selected in the National League expansion draft on October 14. Ten days into the team's inaugural season, the city went wild when Bill Stoneman threw a no-hitter. Gene Mauch, the team's first manager, delivered an unforgettable greeting to a sportswriter when he was introduced to reporters.

"Listen," he said, "if I don't know more about baseball than you do, I've gotta be pretty stupid!" Then he added: "Can you do me a favour? Can you take me to a Canadiens practice tomorrow?" The next morning, Mauch looked down on the Stanley Cup champions

Joseph "Rusty" Staub was one of the big hitters when he played for the Expos from 1969 to 1971 and again in the 1979 season. (GAZETTE-MONTREAL STAR)

Mack Jones in 1969 game against St. Louis. Jones hit a home run, a triple and drove in five runs. (GAZETTE FILES)

Andre Dawson tries to steal second in 1979 but Fernando Gonzalez was there first. (MONTREAL STAR - ADRIAN LUNNY)

Expos' Pete Rose running for a fly ball at Olympic Stadium in 1984. (ANDRÉ PICHETTE)

from a seat high in the Forum. He sat there wordlessly for about 20 minutes. Then, he pointed a finger at one of the players: "That guy can't play on my team," he said. "He's been going through the motions."

"Which guy?"

"The big guy - No. 4," he replied.

"Let's make a deal right now," Mauch was told. "I won't try to tell you anything about baseball, you don't tell me anything about hockey. No. 4 is Jean Béliveau. Maybe you've heard of him."

Alas, Mauch and his Expos finished their first season with a 52-110 record.

The Expos were Rusty Staub, who came to the team from the Houston Astros before the start of its first season for Donn Clendenon and Jesus Alou. They were Gary Carter, Andre Dawson, Larry Walker and Pedro Martinez.

They were a team that appeared headed for a World Series appearance in 1981 until the Dodgers' Rick Monday blasted a winning homer in the ninth inning of the fifth and deciding game of the NL Championship Series at the Olympic Stadium. They were also a team that had the best record in baseball on August 12, 1994, when players walked out, forcing the cancellation of the balance of the season, the playoffs and the World Series. A small consolation was that Felipe Alou was named major league manager of the year.

The rest is all-too-well known: money problems, fire sales involving world-class talents, an Olympic Stadium baseball fans don't want and, sadly, perhaps a team Montrealers don't really care about.

Pedro Martinez pitching in 1995. (GAZETTE - JOHN KENNEY)

Catcher Gary Carter in 1987. (GAZETTE FILES)

Expos manager Felipe Alou in 1999. (GAZETTE - PIERRE OBENDRAUF)

MONTREAL'S CENTURY **95**

The world came to Montreal on July 17, 1976, with all the excitement and glory of the Olympic Games. And for 16 days, audiences would be left breathless by the achievements of the world's best amateur athletes. It was Montreal's biggest sports party of the century, attracting millions of spectators from around the world. It led to a hangover costing billions, but it was great fun while it lasted. (COJO ARCHIVES)

The world came to Montreal on July 17, 1976, with all the pomp and ceremony and celebration of the Games of the XXI Olympiad. Mayor Drapeau had been obsessed with the idea of bringing the Olympics to his city, starting with his first bid to the IOC in 1966 for the 1972 Games, which went to Munich. Four years later, Drapeau had this jewel to add to Montreal's tiara, which by now consisted of the métro, Place des Arts, Expo 67 and the Expos. It didn't come without a price Montrealers would have to pay for decades - and they're still paying. In his bid, Drapeau had convinced the IOC the Games would cost no more than $125 million. His promise: the Games could no more have a deficit than a man could have a baby. Two years later, that heady estimate had grown to $310 million. Then, with cost overruns and construction delays on the Olympic Stadium, it jumped to $1.5 billion.

A crowd of 73,000, including Queen Elizabeth, was there to watch 6,000 athletes from 92 nations parade around Olympic Stadium. And for 16 days, audiences at numerous sites would be left breathless by the achievements of the world's best amateur athletes. Eight world records were set in track, 26 in the pool. It was in Montreal that U.S. boxer Sugar Ray Leonard swept to a gold, where East German swimmer Kornelia Ender, U.S. decathlete Bruce Jenner and the charismatic Soviet weightlifter Vasili Alexeev captivated their audiences, but the XXI Olympiad belonged to an 87-pound, 14-year-old Romanian gymnast named Nadia Comaneci.

The Soviet Union's Olga Korbut, 21, had gone into the Olympics as the reigning queen of gymnastics.

Princess Nadia would leave the Games with seven scores of 10, the first perfect marks in Olympic history. She won the all-around gold medal, two more golds, a silver and a bronze.

The XXI Olympiad belonged to an 87-pound, 14-year-old Romanian gymnast named Nadia Comaneci. She left the Games with seven scores of 10, the first perfect marks in Olympic history. She won the all-around gold medal, two more golds, a silver and a bronze. (COJO Archives)

During the games, eight world records were set in track, 26 in the pool. A crowd of 73,000, including Queen Elizabeth and Prime Minister Pierre Trudeau, was there to watch 6,000 athletes from 92 nations parade around Olympic Stadium. In this picture of the opening ceremonies, the stadium scoreboard shows the Queen and Governor-General Jules Léger. (COJO ARCHIVES)

The Soviet Union's Olga Korbut, 21, had gone into the Montreal Olympics as the reigning queen of gymnastics. A slip of the foot, and the crown was gone. (GAZETTE FILES)

Canadian highjumper Greg Joy raises his arms with pride after a jump that won him a silver medal at the Montreal Olympics. (Le Journal de Montréal – Gilles Lafrance)

Alouettes'
ace flinger Sam
Etcheverry in 1956.
(GAZETTE FILES)

Alouettes quarterback Sonny Wade in 1976. (GAZETTE FILES)

It was Montreal's biggest sports party of the century, attracting millions of spectators from around the world. It led to a hangover costing billions, but it was great fun while it lasted.

More than a half century has passed since the formation of the Montreal Alouettes, a team that has sent 14 of its players and executives to the Canadian Football Hall of Fame. They include Lew Hayman, who took over the team when it was formed in 1946, and who led the Als to the Grey Cup in 1949, one of the four the team was to win.

Also in the Hall are Sam Etcheverry, Hal Patterson, Junior Ah You, George Dixon, Herb Trawick, owner Sam Berger, Terry Evanshen, Marv Lister, Virgil Wagner, Bruce Coulter, Red O'Quinn, Peter Dalla Riva and Gene Gaines. But when you're talking Alouettes football on the field, no two stars shone brighter than quarterback Etcheverry and offensive end Patterson.

Alouettes football was at its entertaining best when both were with the team; no team was quite as exciting even while falling to the Edmonton Eskimos in Grey Cup games from 1954 through '56. Etcheverry was the coach and Sonny Wade the quarterback when the Als won the Grey Cup

The political battle between these two Alouettes fans, Pierre Trudeau and René Lévesque, was much fiercer and much longer than the Grey Cup match they had come to see in 1977. Levesque was accompanied by PQ cabinet ministers Claude Charron and Marcel Léger. (GAZETTE - BRIAN MCINNIS)

Hal Patterson in 1956. (GAZETTE FILES - MONTREAL STAR)

Alouettes star George Dixon performs for the cameras in 1963. (GAZETTE FILES)

Herb Trawick shows off new uniform in 1950. (GAZETTE FILES)

1940s boxing star Johnny Greco showing off his moves for a group of adoring boys. (GAZETTE FILES – MONTREAL STANDARD)

in 1970, Marv Levy its leader when the Als won in 1974 and 1977. Levy went on to coach the NFL Buffalo Bills, and while Joe Scanella was to lead the Als to the Cup final for the next two seasons, they haven't made it back there since.

The Als withdrew from the league in 1982, were promptly granted a new franchise called the Concordes, changed the name back to the Alouettes on the team's 40th anniversary in 1986, then folded in '87. The Als were reborn when the Grey Cup champion Stallions parachuted into Montreal from Baltimore after an ill-conceived CFL marriage of Canadian and U.S. teams and now, after years of fan disinterest and ownership neglect, are attracting sellout crowds to Molson Stadium.

Montrealers with long memories will remember promoter Eddie Quinn, who made wrestling the flavour of the week at the Forum. For years, hardly a Wednesday night went by without main-bout entertainers such as Montreal-born Yvon Robert, and others such as Gorgeous George, Bobby Managoff, Lou Thesz, Wladek Kowalski, Yukon Eric and Don Leo Jonathan filling the place. Robert, needless to say, was the world's heavyweight champion – in Montreal and the rest of the province.

Promoter Quinn, an American, also surrounded himself with an impressive stable of boxers. Dave Castilloux and Johnny Greco were the best of the lot, but no fight before it or since attracted as much attention or was packed with

Wrestling great Yvon Robert argues with the referee during a match in 1945. (Gazette files - Montreal Standard)

Boxer Yvon Durelle chuckles over a photo of a 1958 fight in which he dropped champion Archie Moore three times in the first round. (Gazette files - Montreal Star)

more drama than the one involving Yvon Durelle and world light-heavyweight champion Archie Moore on a December night in 1958.

Durelle was an overwhelming underdog going into this fight. It was a mismatch. But he knocked Moore down three times in the first round, and the fight should have been over the first time the legendary champion was sent crashing to the canvas. The initial damage was done only one minute into the fight when Durelle came out of a crouch with a left hook to Moore's heart, then followed with a right to the chin. Moore froze, then fell heavily. History will note that Moore rose to his feet at the count of nine, but what's also true is that referee Jack Sharkey, a former world heavyweight champion, didn't start his count until four or five seconds had elapsed. The champion got away with a long count, and despite being knocked down again in the fifth, disposed of Durelle in the 11th round.

For Montreal boxing fans, it was truly the fight of the century. ◆

Sellout crowds flock to Jarry Park's DuMaurier Stadium to watch the world's tennis greats compete in the Canadian Open every summer. In this photo, Monica Seles hammers a ball back to Arantxa Sanchez Vicario in the 1996 finals. Seles won the title that year and 3 other years in the late 1990s. (GAZETTE – MARCOS TOWNSEND)

No sport, not even the world's most popular game, soccer, has been able to compete with hockey as Montreal's No. 1 passion. But, as this 1994 photo shows, it's not because soccer lacks excitement. Here, the Impact's Enzo Concina leaps for joy after scoring against the Vancouver 86ers. (LE JOURNAL DE MONTRÉAL – NORMAND PICHETTE)

The speed, the smells, the noise and the crashes. This is the stuff that draws thousands of racing fans to the Canadian Grand Prix in Montreal every year. In this 1998 photo, Alexander Wurz's Benetton flies over Jarno Trulli's Prost-Peugeot in a spectacular crash. No one was injured and Wurz went on to finish in fourth place in his spare car. (ANDRÉ PICHETTE)

Gilles Villeneuve put Quebec on the map of car-racing. He was only 32 when he was killed in a 1982 crash. Above, Villeneuve celebrates his 1978 Montreal Grand Prix victory. The two photos below of the racing legend were shot by André Pichette.

Thumbs up. Like his father before him, Jacques Villeneuve has become an idol and a hero for Quebec car-racing fans. (GAZETTE - PIERRE OBENDRAUF)

In the 1930s, before T.V. entertained sports fans in their livingrooms, people flocked to the mountain to watch ski-jumpers sail above Côte des Neiges. This 1940 photo shows a Montreal Ski Club meet. (GAZETTE FILES)

More than 70 native and adopted Montrealers have represented Canada at Olympic Games and won medals in the past 100 years in individual and team sports. Diver Annie Pelletier (left), seen here with Olympic gold-medalist Sylvie Bernier, won a bronze at the 1996 Games. Here are just a few of the other Montrealers who have brought Olympic glory to their country: Speedskater Nathalie Lambert (gold in 1992 and two silver medals in 1994); synchronized swimmer Sylvie Fréchette (gold in 1992 and silver in 1996); sprinter Bruny Surin of Pierrefonds was part of the relay team that won gold medal in 1996; canoeist Alwyn Morris of Kahnawake (gold and bronze in 1984), boxer Peter Kirby (gold 1964); downhill skier Lucille Wheeler (bronze in 1956); and swimmer George Hodgson (two gold medals in 1912). (GAZETTE - JOHN KENNEY)

Bicycle paths were built along the Lachine Canal in 1977 but it wasn't until the mid-1980s that bike enthusiasts organized the first Tour de l'Île to celebrate the more than 200 km of paths that were completed in 1985. The event has been popular ever since.
(ANDRÉ PICHETTE)

City Mosaic

PEGGY **CURRAN**

O NLY THE FOOLISH BRAVE THE NOISY, clogged traffic on St. Laurent Boulevard, for the Main is a world that is best explored on foot. Chinatown shops give way to the seedy night spots of the red light district. Then, the hip bars and restaurants north of Sherbrooke, past Schwartz's, Moishe's, Warshaw's and Schreter's, Tandoori restaurants and Apollo car repair, Librairie Espanola and the Ukrainian *caisse populaire*, the Portuguese bakery and Copa America, until at last you reach Little Italy and the buzz of the Jean Talon market.

Ida Steinberg opened her store at 4419 St. Laurent in 1917, six years after she emigrated from Hungary to Montreal. This picture, painted by Ben Dobrinsky in 1940, shows the store after it had been enlarged to include the next-door house. The store was the foundation for her family's grocery empire, which lasted 75 years. The Jewish community was growing quickly at the time. By 1924, 12,000 of the 30,000 children enrolled in Montreal's Protestant schools were Jewish.

In the 1940s, a Montreal columnist wrote that "whether you're looking for a gal or a gun, a haircut or a hustler, a hock shop or a hamburger - you'll find it on St. Lawrence Blvd." The prevailing view then, as now, was if you couldn't find it on the Main, it probably wasn't worth having. Today, St. Laurent is no longer the beach that it was at the turn of the century for the waves of immigrants who came to Montreal from Europe. The street is now home to funky boutiques and coffee shops and Montreal's newest residents - from South Asia, Central America, Lebanon and Haiti - are more likely to settle in Côte des Neiges, Villeray, Brossard, Snowdon, Montreal North or St. Laurent. The city mosaic today is more evident in the métro than it is on the trendy Main. Nevertheless, St. Laurent Boulevard was designated a National Historic District in 1998 to mark its role as the first home and meeting place for generations of new Montrealers. It remains the most potent symbol of the amazing transformation that Montreal underwent in the 20th century, from a bustling colonial city with two dominant cultures to a multiethnic metropolis. The typical Montrealer of the year 2000 is less white, more bilingual and better educated than when this century began.

PREVIOUS PAGES

Montreal's rich ethnic diversity is one of the city's greatest charms. For much of this century, Italian was the third most-spoken language after French and English. While Spanish has taken over third spot, the Italian community continues to thrive and, as this photo shows, cheer on Italy's treasured soccer players during the World Cup. (GAZETTE FILES)

Schwartz's on the Main, 1974. (GAZETTE FILES)

We've come a long way from the days of giving birth once a year, baby. Until the 1960s, Quebec's birthrate was among the highest in the world. Families the size of the one Lt. J. Aza Filiatreault sired were not uncommon, although his was the largest for a member of the Montreal police department in 1940 when this photo was taken. Seated in the centre of the group is Filiatreault, flanked by his mother and his second wife (right). Around him are 18 of his 20 children living at the time; newborn twin girls were missing from the photo. Filiatreault's first wife bore 12 children before her death 13 years earlier. Two died, as did one of his 11 children by his second wife. By the end of the century, Quebec's birthrate was among the lowest in Canada. (Gazette files)

In 1900, there was no dispute over the social event of the fall season in English Montreal. Though Scots made up the smallest segment of Montreal's English-speakers – both the English and Irish communities were bigger – the Scottish influence was felt from the banks on St. James Street to the parlours of the Square Mile, a neighbourhood whose residents controlled 70 per cent of Canada's wealth. All the best people gathered at the Windsor Hotel in late November for the annual St. Andrew's Ball, which featured bagpipers, Annie Laurie punch

and "a boar's head with real tusks ornamented with sugar... lifelike to the last degree."

On the other side of the tracks, Montreal was a different city. At the turn of the century, historian Terry Copp wrote in *The Anatomy of Poverty*, the typical Montreal family consisted of "a married couple with three children who lived in a five-room, cold-water flat on a narrow, densely populated side street in what is now the inner core of the city." In 1901, the annual income of an unskilled male labourer was $405.

While H.L. Putnam advertised "cheap,

Immigration has brought the colours, music and flavours of the Caribbean to city neighbourhoods. At no time is that more in evidence than during the Carifiesta parade, where the costumes dazzle and music massages the soul. (GAZETTE - SHANE KELLEY)

Irish eyes are smiling in Montreal every year at the St. Patrick's Day parade when thousands turn out to celebrate the Irish. On March 17, everyone loves green. (LE JOURNAL DE MONTRÉAL - ALBERT VINCENT)

There were few playgrounds in the city in 1925, when this photo was taken, and children shared the streets with a growing number of cars. It wasn't until the Great Depression that playgrounds were built in large numbers, part of Mayor Camillien Houde's massive public works program. (GAZETTE FILES - MONTREAL STAR)

Montreal's song is one of diversity. Daniel McGrowder (right), Helen Gatama (centre) and Samantha Mills sang their hearts out with the Joybells Children's Choir at Westmount's Seventh Day Adventist Church during the annual Christmas concert in 1996. (GAZETTE – PHIL CARPENTER)

This little girl watched the Greek National Day parade in 1996 through the legs of members of the Greek presidential national guard. (GAZETTE – JOHN KENNEY)

modern cottages" in Westmount for $4,000, living conditions in other parts of town were less than ideal. In 1897, businessman Herbert Brown Ames published The City Below the Hill, in which he detailed what life was like for 38,000 people in districts such as Point St. Charles, St. Henri and Griffintown.

Only 27 of 178 miles of streets in the area were paved. There were 3,000 horse stables and 500 cow barns within city limits. Most city water was untreated and unfiltered, and garbage was dumped in lanes. At least 5,000 households still used outhouses, despite the fact that privies were illegal. Though on the decline, the city's death rate was among the highest in the civilized world. Between 1899 and 1901, one in four babies died before its first birthday, a rate which was higher than any city except Calcutta. Infant

deaths accounted for 43 per cent of all recorded deaths in 1897. (As late as 1926, Montreal's infant mortality rate was 14 per cent, almost double that of New York or Toronto.) Quebec's birth rate was among the highest in the world. Montreal's population doubled from 1881 to 1901 and doubled again between 1901 and 1911, in large part because of high birth rates.

Back in 1901, Montreal society could be broken down into two main language groups. More than 95 per cent of the city's population was either French- or English-speaking. People of British and Irish background made up 38 per cent of Montreal's population. Montreal's French community had been growing since before Confederation and Montreal was becoming more French than it had been in the 19th century. By the early 1900s, there were small Italian,

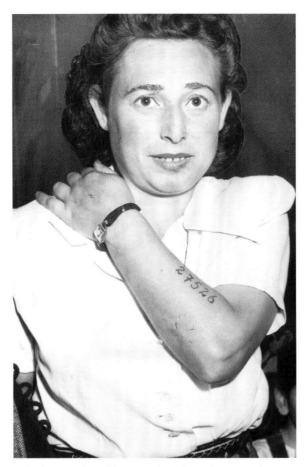

The horrors of World War II brought a change to the racist immigration laws that kept non-whites and many Jews out of Canada for much of the first half of the century. Bella Rappaport, one of thousands of concentration camp survivors and displaced persons to come to Canada after the war, arrived in Montreal in 1947 with her husband. She stayed with her brother on De Bullion Street. (GAZETTE FILES)

Displaced family sees its new city for the first time in 1947. (GAZETTE FILES - MONTREAL STAR)

Greek and other European communities. Montreal had had a small Jewish community dating back to the 1760s, when a handful of men founded Canada's first synagogue, Shearith Israel (now the Spanish and Portuguese synagogue). But it was growing, as Jews fled persecution in Czarist Russia. Most were poor. As late as 1931, only 252 of Montreal's 60,000 Jews listed English as their mother tongue.

As their numbers grew, Jewish immigrants moved up the St. Laurent corridor, the north-south artery which came to be seen as a linguistic divide between English- and French-speaking Montreal.

Though they were not welcomed with open arms, European immigrants could be thankful they weren't treated as the Chinese were - with open hostility and racism. In 1900, The Gazette wrote that a $50 laundry tax "kept many an anxious Chink making deep dives into the Chinese sock in which he had placed his pile."

Since 1885, after the national railroad was completed, Chinese immigrants had been subject to a head tax. The high tax, which was $500 in 1923, made it next to impossible for men to send for their wives and children. Chinatown was a world of men. In 1901, there were 1,033 Chinese men and four Chinese women in Montreal; as late as 1951, the male-female ratio was 3-to-1. The head tax was abolished in 1923 and was replaced by a ban on Chinese immigration until 1947.

Three centuries after Matthew da Costa arrived as Samuel de Champlain's translator in 1606, Montreal's black community was still small and close-knit, with nine out of 10 black Montrealers living around St. Antoine Street in an area then known as the Montreal Negro district or "Sporting District." In 1902, a handful of strong-willed American women who had come north with their railway porter husbands took charge of community affairs. They set up the Coloured Women's Club, which would play

*The Chin children arrived in the city in 1951. (*GAZETTE FILES*)*

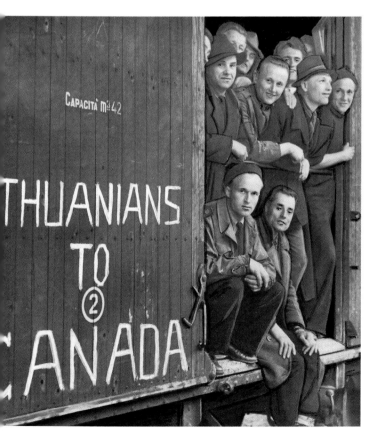

*These Lithuanians arrived in 1948. They were among 860 Balkan and Baltic nationals who survived war camps in Germany and came to Montreal for a new life. (*GAZETTE FILES*)*

*Jewish immigrants who had fled Spain in 1944 were greeted by tearful Montreal relatives on their arrival by train. (*GAZETTE FILES*)*

A Tibetan woman and child on their arrival in 1971 from India, where the family had lived as refugees for 10 years. They were among 17 Tibetan refugees who arrived that day, more than a decade after they fled Chinese persecution in their homeland. (MONTREAL STAR – GERRY DAVIDSON)

a key role in the establishment of the Union Church and the Negro Community Centre. When land owners set exorbitant prices for blacks who wanted to buy their own homes, a community association bought large lots and sold it back at fair market rates.

But the black community's ability to grow was stymied by official and unofficial obstacles. The 1910 Immigration Act restricted non-white immigration to Canada on the pretext that people of other races "do not assimilate well and cannot adapt themselves to our climatic conditions."

McGill University did not accept blacks to study law or medicine. In 1928, a former CPR porter and war veteran named Rufus Rockhead was the first black to be granted a liquor licence in Montreal – but not before he was told to forget about running a tavern in a "white" district. For decades, Rockhead's Paradise Café showcased jazz and blues greats like Cab Calloway, Sarah Vaughan and Ella Fitzgerald on their way up the ladder.

As an industrial and manufacturing centre, Montreal was especially hard hit by the Great Depression and in turn, hard times strained tolerance for the city's rapidly growing immigrant neighbourhoods.

Locally and internationally, nationalism and anti-Semitism were the flavours of the day. Abbé Lionel Groulx urged readers and followers to boycott Jewish businesses. "If we do not buy from the Jews, they will leave." But anti-Semitism was not restricted to ethnic purists like Groulx. In 1931, Canada passed a new immigration law that specifically excluded Jews. Three years later, students at the Université de Montréal went on strike to prevent Samuel Rabinovitch from entering medical school. In the Laurentians, signs posted at clubs and beaches told the story: "Jews are not wanted here in Ste. Agathe, so scram while the going is good."

McGill University also practiced discrimination against Jews. Until 1956, it restricted admission of Jewish students by requiring them to have higher averages than other entrants.

The horrors of World War II brought a shift in attitudes on several fronts. The year 1947 finally brought an end to the Chinese Exclusion Act and the resumption of Jewish immigration;

Montreal eventually claimed one of the highest concentrations of Holocaust survivors anywhere. Black veterans earned the respect and rights they had sought for their community. When the Brooklyn Dodgers sent Jackie Robinson to play for their Montreal Royals farm team, the city welcomed him.

Canada eliminated race quotas from its immigration policy in 1962, easing the way for West Indian, Haitian and Filipino immigrants. From the Hungarian revolution of 1956 to Pinochet's Chilean coup in 1973 to the recent conflict in Kosovo, political upheaval has brought fresh waves of refugees and exiles to Montreal from every continent. As war raged in Vietnam, thousands of young American men crossed the border to avoid the draft. Once the war ended, boatloads of refugees from southeast Asia sought

Vietnamese refugee To Chi Miuh arrived at Montreal International Airport - Mirabel in 1979. (GAZETTE - TEDD CHURCH)

Vaishali Raja, 18 months, a Ugandan refugee, struggles with her luggage as she and her family arrive in Montreal. (GAZETTE FILES)

Hasidic Jews have settled in several areas, in particular Outremont.
(Gazette – Gordon Beck)

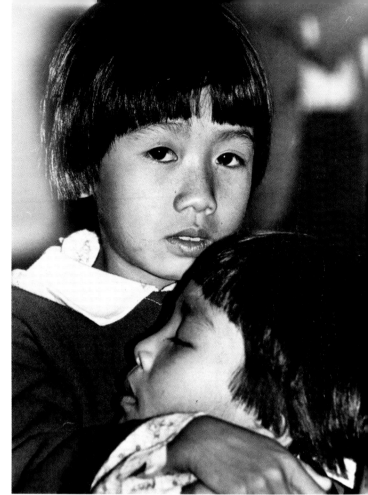

Vietnam was a long way away for these two little refugees in 1979. (Gazette - John Mahoney)

asylum in the west. Since 1975, about 20,000 Cambodians have settled in Canada, almost half of them coming to Montreal. Half the new immigrants to Quebec in the last 15 years have been Asians. According to the Montreal Island School Council, 160 languages can be heard in city schoolyards.

Despite extraordinary changes to the ethnic mix, the first half of the century saw little shift in English-French relations, which could be described at best as cool. "Between the two races, French and English so different in mentality and methods, there exists a cordiality that rather surprises outsiders," Charles W. Stokes wrote in Here and There in Montreal in 1924. "They do not intermarry to any particular degree, and they do not pretend to like the other race better than their own." Indeed, the conscription crisis of 1942 demonstrated just

how differently the two communities viewed the world. The Quiet Revolution of the 1960s and French Quebec's abrupt shift away from the church spelled a new era for Montrealers. The city, which socially and economically had been dominated for so long by the English was about to change hands. Within two decades, the francophone middle class had become more educated, the Parti Québécois had passed laws favouring francophones and thousands of anglophones and the business and industries they controlled left. Socially and economically, francophones had become *maîtres chez nous.*

Non-francophones who stayed have evolved with the times. The vast majority is bilingual. Many send their children to French or immersion schools. As the century wound down, there were more intermarriages, more ethnically diverse neighbourhoods and better

The celebration of the feast of Holy Christ of Miracles in 1983 attracted many in the Portuguese community. (GAZETTE - GORDON BECK)

ethnic restaurants and cultural events than ever before in Montreal. Life in the city is spicier and, in many ways, better.

Montreal now has one of the lowest infant mortality rates in the world, second only to Japan and Ireland. A typical Montrealer can expect to live to 79 - 10 years longer than life expectancy in 1957.

These days, only one in four Montrealers lays claim to an English, Scots or Irish ancestor. Spanish has overtaken Italian as Montreal's third language. While the Jewish community has shrunk from 120,000 in the 70s to about 100,000, it ranks among the strongest in North America.

A new generation of trilingual Montrealers is reshaping the city's linguistic boundaries. Immigrants from around the world now make up more than 30 per cent of the population of St. Laurent, Ahuntsic, Côte St. Luc, St. Léonard, Dollard des Ormeaux and Town of Mount Royal, with large concentrations in Laval, Longueuil, Brossard and Greenfield Park.

In *Montréal, Une société multiculturelle*, Claire McNicoll suggests Montreal's duel heritage may have paved the way for the successful integration of immigrants, making the city a model of peaceful coexistence of many ethnic groups.

Walk the streets of the city. You can see how, in the past 100 years, generations of new Montrealers have left their marks on the city and found a home in neighbourhoods old and new. ◆

Show Time

BILL **BROWNSTEIN**

WHAT A DIFFERENCE a bunch of decades can make. Yeah. In this town,
we could sing and dance to such
a refrain, and we probably will.

Politics, economics and culture have dra-
matically changed the face of Montreal over
the last century. Yet one aspect of city life has
remained unaltered: in spite of all the divisions
and ever-fluctuating demographics, Montreal
is still the party capital of Canada – not that it
is always immediately obvious why we should
be celebrating.

During the latter decades of the century, Montreal has gained a reputation as a city of festivals, led by the world-renowned Montreal International Jazz Festival, which celebrated its 20th anniversary in 1999. Shown here is but a fraction of the crowd at the main outdoor concert of the 1993 edition. (GAZETTE – GORDON BECK)

PREVIOUS PAGES

Forget any politicians that have sprung from these parts, or any captains of industry. No Quebecer this century has achieved greater global renown than the sweetheart of Charlemagne, pop diva Céline Dion. Her records have sold in the tens of millions and her concert tours have drawn hundreds of thousands. She is also a walking advertisement for the rewards of bilingualism: already a star in Quebec, her career soared into the international stratosphere when she began singing in English as well as French. (GAZETTE – ANDRÉ PICHETTE)

Burlesque queen Lili St. Cyr is the reigning symbol of Montreal's "sin city" era of the 1940s and '50s. Her striptease shows at the storied Gayety Theatre made her Montreal's most famous woman of the age, and while her stage persona was steeped in Gay-Paree fantasy, she was born Marie Klarquist in Minneapolis. She was 81 when she died in February 1999. (GAZETTE FILES)

Granted, the Sin City of the postwar 1940s has given way to today's relatively more sanitized Céline City. Actually, with no disrespect intended for chart-busting supersinger Céline Dion, Festival City might even be a more apt description for Montreal. As its citizens are well aware, Montreal has more festivals per capita than anywhere else on the face of the planet. We pay homage to jazz, comedy, film, fireworks, French song, beer, bratwurst, bugs, lobster, dragon boats, winter and souvlaki with a fervour that is as endearing as it is alarming to both locals and tourists.

Indeed, Céline is about the only institution without a festival in her honour. Which is odd, considering that she is merely the most successful cultural export to have ever emerged from these parts.

In the bad old days, there were no festivals on the streets. Folks had to make do with other forms of entertainment, some more risqué than others as the century unfolded.

Times change. In lieu of Sammy Davis Jr.,
Jerry Lewis or Frank Sinatra swaggering down
the Main, their booze, babes and posses in tow,
we now have Eddie Murphy, John Travolta and
Bruce Willis swaggering down the Main, their
personal trainers, food-blenders and posses in
tow. The former entertainers came to whoop it
up at the legendary nightclubs of yesteryear,
while the latter are among a growing group of
health-conscious luminaries who have come to
make their movies here in Hollywood North,
where the U.S. buck buys a whole whack more.

In lieu of Lili St. Cyr titillating wide-eyed
troops returning from battle overseas and entire
rosters of visiting professional sports squads, we
now have legions of no-name but fresh-faced
lap-dancers titillating wide-eyed tourists and
entire rosters of visiting sports squads.

In lieu of illicit barbotte card games being
played at blind pigs, we now have legal black-
jack being played at the Montreal Casino.

The bebop masters of yore have given way

*Montrealers have held their own on the stage of the local jazz
fest with the best in the world. Two of Montreal's towering musical talents, jazz pianist Oliver Jones and singing star Ginette
Reno, share a laugh at the 1993 festival.* (GAZETTE – RICHARD
ARLESS)

Members of a heavenly choir, Montreal's celebrated Jubilation Gospel Choir raised the roof at Place des Arts during a 1998 jazz festival performance before a typical sellout crowd. (GAZETTE – ALLEN McINNIS)

to a new breed of hipster at the Montreal International Jazz Festival. The vaudevillians of yore have given way to the cutups at the Juste pour rire/Just for Laughs comedy festival. And the moral crusaders of yore... well, they've all but disappeared with the passing of the barbotte games, blind pigs and the lovely Lili St. C.

Fact is: just about everything is aboveboard today, and the various levels of government are only too willing to share the tax spoils accrued from gaming and alcohol consumption. More to the point, in their efforts to ensure that the revelry is nonstop, the various levels of government grant generous subsidies to the myriad festivals and offer incentives to film and TV producers in order that their wads of cash are spent here.

Yet, as was the case during the days of darling Lili, entertainment dollars go a long way toward stoking Montreal's economic engine,

not to mention nurturing the soul of the city.

It wasn't always this festive here. In turn-of-the-century Montreal, the barons of industry belonged to the Anglo-Scottish establishment. And while powerful clans cut the rug at their lavish balls, the city they virtually ruled tended to be staid and God-fearing.

World War I and then the Great Depression also put a damper on excessive partying here – as it did almost everywhere else. Then again, getting a drink and - er - a good time in Montreal has never been problematic to those willing to pursue.

At the beginning of the century, those in the know could kick up their heels at the Recreation Key Club, a jazz joint on St. Antoine Street, or later at the Nemderoloc – "colored men" spelled backward – Owl and Terminal clubs. It was at the Terminal where a young hoofer called Sammy Davis Jr. got his start,

The annual FrancoFolies festival showcases French-speaking talent from Quebec and the rest of the French-speaking world. Chanteuse Nathalie Choquette is shown here performing with the Montreal Symphony Orchestra at an outdoor concert in 1999. (GAZETTE – ALLEN MCINNIS)

working with his father and uncle in the Will Mastin Trio. But the city's most renowned jazz establishment of them all, Rockhead's Paradise Café, opened its doors in 1928 and thrived until the '50s.

And prior to the peeling Lili St. Cyr, there was the lovely and talented and enterprising Texas Guinan. In lieu of taking it off, Tex mostly opted to crack wise at the Frolics Café on the Main, and bring new meaning to the Roaring '20s. Tex's trademark call "Hello, suckers!" proved prophetic. She was making $30,000 a month during those cash-strapped times. Harry Houdini also roared here, but, alas, Montreal was also the magician's last pitstop. He suffered a mortal injury after a McGill University student punched him in the stomach during a show at the Princess Theatre.

The onset of World War II saw Montreal become a centre for the war industries, partic-

Her Majesty might not be amused, but the rest of us are. Second only to the jazz festival in drawing power and as a globally renowned showcase is Montreal's annual Juste pour rire/Just for Laughs comedy festival. Here, festival founder Gilbert Rozon mugs with a larger-than-life caricature of Queen Elizabeth. (GAZETTE – GORDON BECK)

The British invasion, 20th-century style. Redcoats were out and mop-tops were in as the Beatles took Montreal and the rest of the continent by storm during their first North American tour in 1964. In this photo, the unidentified lucky winner of a radio station contest presents a long telegram of welcome to (from left) Ringo Starr, George Harrison, Paul McCartney and John Lennon. (MONTREAL STAR–ADRIAN LUNNY)

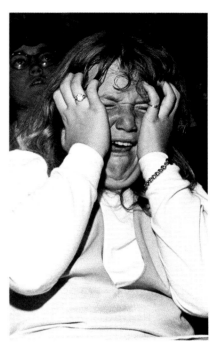

Montrealers were no more immune to Beatlemania than other North Americans. Here, a mercifully unidentified fan shows the classic symptoms at the Fab Four's September 1964 Forum concert. (MONTREAL STAR – ADRIAN LUNNY)

ularly aircraft production. With this prosperity and with the city also being a centre for Allied troops between assignment, all complemented by the permissiveness favoured by Mayor Camillien Houde, the elements were soon in place for unprecedented hell-raisin'.

By the mid-1940s, the captains of vice were giving the barons of industry a run for their money and vying for the best tables at Ruby Foo's, the city's premier resto and place to be seen. Betting parlours and bawdy houses abounded, and Montreal had little difficulty living up to its billing as Sin City. As war ended, the club scene also boomed. On any given night, folks could catch Frank Sinatra or Dean Martin crooning at the Chez Paree, Gene Krupa bang-

ing his drums all night long at Chez Maurice Danceland, Mahalia Jackson bringing the house down at Her Majesty's Theatre, Édith Piaf singing her aching heart out at the Sans Souci, and Jerry Lewis actually keeping his mouth shut in a pantomime shtick at the Esquire.

However, it wasn't the many celebs but rather a buxom young lady from Minneapolis who was most associated with Montreal's bubbling nightlife during the '40s and early '50s. Her name was actually Marie Klarquist, but she was

The laureate of beautiful losers, poet, pop troubadour and Zen traveller. Leonard Cohen has been the epitome of Montreal cool since the 1960s, when his "Suzanne" took us down to a place by the river. (GAZETTE – DAVE SIDAWAY)

Folk chansonnier Gilles Vigneault, a native of Natashquan on Quebec's rugged Lower North Shore, was one of the leading voices of the new Québécois culture that emerged with the Quiet Revolution. His signature tune, Gens du pays, was adopted as Quebec's unofficial national anthem in the 1970s. (GAZETTE – PIERRE OBENDRAUF)

"Québec Love, ça c'est mon bag." Seminal Quebec rocker Robert Charlebois shows classic rock'n'roll attitude (and hairstyle) in a 1969 performance of his legendary Osstidcho *concert tour. His visceral blend of Québécois slang and Chuck Berry chops heralded the emergence of a new cultural force in Quebec.* (MONTREAL STAR – GEORGE BIRD)

better known to her legions of bug-eyed fans as Lili St. Cyr. She became Montreal's most famous woman, simply by stripping with such exotic panache at the Gayety Theatre.

Tame though Lili might be by today's lap-dancing standards, the new morality was a bit much for crusading police chief Pacifique "Pax" Plante and young crown prosecutor Jean Drapeau. By the mid-'50s, they succeeded in bringing this roller-coaster ride to a halt. The party continued, but it was much more subdued as Drapeau turned his attention to becoming mayor and making Montreal a world-class city. He gave us the métro, Expo 67 and the 1976 Olympic Games, and, oy, did he give us debt for our newfound sophistication.

Not that the music died. Far from it. Montreal teens lapped up the British invasion like their counterparts from around the world and gave the Beatles the royal treatment at the Forum and the Rolling Stones at the Maurice Richard Arena in the early '60s. Bob Dylan's protest tunes found attentive young ears at the New Penelope Café. The wicked Wilson Pickett, the Four Tops and Joe Tex let loose with the R&B at the Esquire Show Bar. Local boy Leonard Cohen dazzled the denizens, particularly the ladies, with his poetry, and wowed the rest of the world with musical interpretations of his art. (If Dylan could become a singing sensation, why not our Lenny?) John Lennon proved he could make music - and peace - in a Queen Elizabeth Hotel bed with tone-deaf mate, Yoko Ono. And the '60s also made superstars of homegrown crooning talent like Robert Charlebois and Diane Dufresne.

Yet while the young and restless let their freak-flags fly at the Swiss Hut and while the bohemians tweaked their mustaches and chain-smoked their Gitanes at the bistros of Mountain, Stanley and St. Denis streets in the '60s and early '70s, it must also be noted, sadly to some, that disco did rule in this period at clubs like the Don Juan. And yes, that was the globe-trotting Liz and Dick who chose to tie the knot, neither for the first time, here at the Ritz. That's Taylor and Burton for all you post-boomer kids.

During this epoch, would-be intellectuals and industrialists alike converged at the Boiler Room and Sir Winston Churchill Pub on Crescent Street. Yes, before the swank restos and hotspots on the Main and St. Denis were all the rage, Crescent Street was the place to be and the source of countless careers, relationships, bogus sociology theses, legit prose and chronic liver conditions.

But by the mid-'70s and early '80s,

Diane Dufresne, the Grande Dame of Quebec rock, in a 1974 pose. Imagine Janis Joplin raised on Édith Piaf. (GAZETTE FILES – MONTREAL STAR)

By the time of this 1980 photo, Luc Plamondon had already established himself as the premier Quebec songwriter of his generation, a standing he would enhance in years to come. His hit musicals, such as Starmania *and* Notre-Dame de Paris, *made him Quebec's answer to Andrew Lloyd Webber.* (GAZETTE – TEDD CHURCH)

no amount of carousing could blot the spectre of separation and the subsequent exodus of industry and anglos, mostly down the 401. Montrealers of all stripes sobered up in a jiff and stopped to lick their wounds. The clinking of the birdbath martini glasses almost ceased at the Beaver Club. Skeptics concluded that the party was finally over, and all that remained was for someone to turn out the lights.

But, no. Our pioneering party spirit managed to prevail. Besides, misery loves company.

And a festival in which to drown our sorrows.

We mutter and moan about the inordinate number of festivals Montreal plays host to annually. But they give us purpose and a party. They give half the city – or it so seems – steady employment, either staffing or commenting on the fests. And they give everyone else an excuse to celebrate until they drop and without an iota of guilt.

But mostly the festivals serve one precious function: they give us a reprieve from real life.

Piano man extraordinaire Oscar Peterson came out of Montreal's Little Burgundy neighbourhood to achieve world recognition as one of the all-time giants of jazz. (Gazette – Allen McInnis)

Politics are absolutely lost in a maze of beery good vibes on the streets. Harsh winters and economic woes are forgotten. Same, too, with the Montreal Canadiens' startling demise.

And Montreal metamorphoses into the party town that launched Lili St. Cyr. And on occasion, citizens can even reassure one another with that age-old "ain't life grand" mantra.

Even if it ain't. Self-deception isn't necessarily a sin, and it often beats the alternative. ◆

When Charlie Biddle came to Montreal it was to play, not to stay. But a few dates stretched into decades, and in the course he has weathered into the patriarch of Montreal's jazz scene — and of a family whose second generation is making a mark on the city. (Gazette – Gordon Beck)

Encore Encore

ARTHUR **KAPTAINIS**

W HO WOULD HAVE TAKEN Montreal, at the turn of the last century, for a festival city in the making? It was a port town and rail terminus, smelling of steel, grain and sweat, a place where fortunes were made. The anglophone and francophone establishments – however they disagreed on points of sacred and social doctrine – shared at least a mistrust of those useless avocations understood collectively to be the arts.

Yet with the acquisition of wealth comes the urge to spend it well, and while the workers

Montrealers have an ongoing love affair with the standing ovation. Les Grands Ballets Canadiens' prima ballerina Andrea Boardman stands with classical grace amid the seats of Place Wilfrid Pelletier, from which many an audience has leaped in praise of her turns onstage. (GAZETTE – ALLEN MCINNIS)

Ludmilla Chiriaeff, the godmother of dance in Montreal, founded Les Grands Ballets Canadiens in 1958.

of the city were still preoccupied with subsistence, a vigorous middle class was taking shape. Thus the snowy acres south of Mount Royal became, artistically, the most arable of lands. Our fundamental growths, inherited from Britain and France, could flourish and form hybrids, to which immigration would add strains of infinite variety.

Take the Montreal Symphony Orchestra, founded in 1935 by French-Canadian malcontents who could no longer abide the Montreal Orchestra, or more specifically, its director,

The Montreal Symphony Orchestra finished the century under the direction of Swiss-born Charles Dutoit, who elevated it to international repute during his tenure. He is accompanied here by Italian supermezzo Cecilia Bartoli, who guested at a 1997 MSO fundraiser. (Gazette – André Pichette)

Charles Dutoit took over the artistic direction of the Montreal Symphony Orchestra in 1977 and turned it into one of the world's finest. Under his direction, the MSO has more than 75 recordings to its credit. In this 1987 photo (left), about 50,000 Montrealers showed up at Ahuntsic Park for a free outdoor concert. (Gazette – George Bird)

Douglas Clarke. This redoubtable Englishman would sooner have conducted topless than give a certain young francophone maestro, Wilfrid Pelletier, access to the podium. Among the objectives of the new organization was to provide a forum for French-Canadian soloists and composers, and it was noted with pride that Plateau Hall, its home, was a facility of the east end. In fact, the new orchestra and the Clarke band used the same rank-and-file musicians.

Music being a universal language, the Société des Concerts Symphoniques de Montréal (as it was then called) lost its French character almost in inverse proportion to its artistic advances. Pelletier himself spoke English as fluently as he did French. By 1953, the orchestra, enriched by wartime refugees and supported by cultivated immigrants, was renamed bilingually as the Orchestre Symphonique de Montréal/Montreal Symphony Orchestra. (Although the current administration refuses to acknowledge the English name, it has never fallen out of use.) Zubin Mehta, music director from 1961-67, usually rehearsed in English. By

The name of Wilfrid Pelletier lives on in the main concert hall of Montreal's Place des Arts, named after him in 1966, three years after its construction. Pelletier established the classics in Montreal when he set up the Concerts Symphoniques de Montréal in 1935, which evolved into the Montreal Symphony Orchestra. Pelletier, shown here with his wife, opera singer Rose Brampton, went on to conduct the orchestra of the Metropolitan Opera Company in New York City. A lesser-known distinction is that in his days as a curly haired pre-adolescent, he played the role of French Canadians' patron saint in St. Jean Baptiste Day parades. (GAZETTE FILES – THE STANDARD)

the 1970s the MSO was perceived, and in certain quarters condemned, as a substantially anglophone institution. Yet the genius of Charles Dutoit, the debonair Swiss conductor hired in 1977, was to cultivate and promote the MSO internationally as an ensemble with a special aptitude for French repertoire. In the unforgettable words of a British critic, "The finest French orchestra today, whatever they think in Paris."

There was music in Montreal before the MSO, especially opera. It is with a slack jaw today that we read of Pietro Mascagni conducting his own works in the Montreal Arena in 1902 and the Metropolitan Opera under Arturo Toscanini visiting His Majesty's Theatre

in 1911. Pelletier gave the downbeat of Gounod's *Roméo et Juliette* at Loews not long before midnight on May 7, 1931, after the usual variety offerings had run their course. Possibly some patrons witnessed both shows. This was an age when the demarcation between middle-brow and highbrow was not so clear, particularly where the voice was concerned.

It has become a staple of Montreal arts lore that francophones are drawn to l'art lyrique – as singing is grandiloquently known – while the anglos prefer the symphony. The canard is hard to substantiate. There were two major amateur choral societies in the early part of the century, the Montreal Elgar Choir and Les Disciples de Massenet, each named after the leading musi-

For much of the century, women were rigidly excluded from established symphony orchestras, no matter how well they might play. Montreal violinist Ethel Stark (inset) fought back by organizing the all-woman Montreal Women's Symphony Orchestra in 1940. The ground-breaking ensemble endured more than two decades and became the first Canadian symphony orchestra to play New York City's Carnegie Hall. (GAZETTE FILES)

cal taste-maker of the motherland. The St. Lawrence Choir, attached informally to the MSO, started in the West Island but has evolved, under Iwan Edwards, into a linguistically equitable organism. Opera, to be sure, has always had a strong francophone following, although the anglophone soprano Pauline Donalda presented 28 seasons of opera in the middle of the century. Performers have come from both camps. Among males, tenor André Turp and bass Joseph Rouleau acquired international fame in French roles, while Louis Quilico became one of the great Verdi baritones of his generation. Contralto Maureen Forrester is probably the most famous of all musical Montrealers (despite having moved, like Quilico, to Toronto). While

all of the above found themselves singing outside their city more often than in it, there were attempts after the 1960s (possibly spurred by the breathtaking operatic programming of Expo 67) to establish a serious opera house. The deficit-plagued Opéra du Québec was supplanted in 1980 by the Opéra de Montréal. Led by a dynamic bottom-liner, Bernard Uzan, this company – resident, like the MSO, in the acoustically so-so Place des Arts – has attracted variable notices but loyal crowds.

Instrumentalists also have flourished in the city, thanks to the duplication fostered by multiple teaching institutions – which brings us again to the unique dynamic of two languages at work. The Conservatoire de Musique du

Louis Lortie is perhaps Montreal's best-known classical pianist of the century. He was 13 (inset) when he played his first Beethoven concerto with the Montreal Symphony Orchestra in 1972. (GAZETTE FILES)

Québec à Montréal, founded by Pelletier, was modeled after its state-sponsored namesake in Paris. The Ecole Vincent-D'Indy, operated by nuns, was where Yvonne Hubert generated a bumper crop of pianists, including Marc-André Hamelin, André Laplante, Louis Lortie and Janina Fialkowska. McGill University, whose music faculty was reorganized by the German draft-dodger Helmut Blume, has become famous for its orchestral and opera programs. Even in the 1940s, there were enough players in town to fuel the Montreal Women's Symphony Orchestra, established and led by a Montreal violinist, Ethel Stark.

With strong composition departments at both McGill and the Université de Montréal,

Yuli Turovzky, shown here with daughter Natalya and wife Eleonora in 1987, is the heart of I Musici de Montreal. (GAZETTE - JOHN MAHONEY)

the city is a breeding ground for composers. Not much music by such pre-modern Montrealers as Claude Champagne and Alexis Contant remains in the active repertoire, but Pierre Mercure, born in 1927 and killed in a auto accident less than 39 years later, wrote enduringly bright and modern orchestral scores. Jean Papineau-Couture, Gilles Tremblay (not born in Montreal, but an early migrant) and Claude Vivier have made lasting contributions. Among anglos native to the city, the octogenarian Alexander Brott can pride himself in a neo-classical corpus that has aged well. He is known also as the conductor of the McGill Chamber Orchestra, an orchestra that has faced stiff competition since the 1980s from I Musici de Montréal, led by expatriate Russian cellist Yuli Turovsky. Like the MSO, the Turovsky group is known to the wide world through CDs on a British recording label. Two chamber-music societies, the Ladies' Morning Musical Club and Pro Musica, reflect, though no longer uphold, their Westmount and Outremont ori-

Alexander Brott (left) with his musical wife, Lotte, and sons Denis (playing cello) and Boris in a 1960s photo. (GAZETTE FILES)

Edwin Holgate's Great Bog Pond, Cache Rive, *1939.* (Gazette files)

gins. All those churches Mark Twain noticed when he visited Montreal have fostered a vigorous local organ culture. Add to this a clutch of baroque ensembles, some domestic recording companies, the radio forces of the CBC in two languages, and you have a music scene that would service a town of twice the population.

The linguistic divide has not been so deep in the realm of visual arts, for the good reason that most anglophone Montreal painters at the turn of the century – William Bymner and Maurice Cullen being examples – were smitten by France. Collectors and critics did not necessarily share this sympathy. "Post-Impressionism is a fad," prophesied Samuel Morgan-Powell in the Montreal Star after a 1913 show. "London is laughing today at the latest freak of Matisse... If Montreal joins hands

Artist Edwin Holgate was a founding member of the Beaver Hall Group in 1920. (GAZETTE-JEAN-PIERRE RIVEST)

Artist John Lyman dealt with the Montreal art scene by moving to Paris. (GAZETTE FILES)

Stanley Cosgrove was a founding member of the Contemporary Arts Society in the 1930s. This 1996 photo captured Cosgrove in his studio with Jeune Femme Assise. (GAZETTE-JOHN MAHONEY)

MONTREAL'S CENTURY **147**

Prudence Heward's painting Two Women at the Theatre. (GAZETTE FILES)

with London and laughs, the craze will soon pass."

It was partly this atmosphere that drove A.Y. Jackson from his home town to similarly ossified Toronto, where he at least found kindred spirits in the other members of the Group of Seven. James Wilson Morrice and his disciple John Lyman dealt with the Montreal problem by exiling themselves for long periods, mostly in Paris. Other anglophone francophiles formed a collective in 1920 called the Beaver Hall Group. This included Edwin Holgate, who, despite his preference for portrait over landscape, was eventually named the eighth member of the Group of Seven. Prudence Heward was the best of the women painters of Montreal in the first half of the century, and Lilias Torrence Newton enjoyed wide success as a portraitist of

the rich and famous. Paradoxically, some of the Montreal painters least influenced by European trends were francophones. Ozias Leduc, a church decorator who painted luminous still lifes and symbolic canvases in modest seclusion in nearby Saint-Hilaire, has acquired a saintly mystique since his death in 1955. Marc-Aurèle Fortin painted the port of Montreal as well as rustic landscapes with almost primitive individualism.

Morrice ended his days in Tunis, but Lyman returned in 1931, restarting his career as a painter-propagandist and conceiving a strong dislike for the supposedly reactionary Group of Seven. By 1939, he had formed the Contemporary Arts Society, which was open to all artists of "non-academic tendencies." There was room among the founding 25 members for the anglo post-impressionists Stanley Cosgrove and Goodridge Roberts, the Great Depression chroniclers Louis Muhlstock and Marian Scott, and others with more radical agendas, notably Paul-Émile Borduas. This abstract painter and his followers (Marcel Barbeau, Léon Bellefleur, Roger Fauteux, Pierre Gauvreau, Fernand Leduc, Jean-Paul Mousseau and Jean-Paul Riopelle) soon struck out on their own. A Borduas canvas – Automatisme 1.47 – suggested to critic Tancrède Marsil a nickname: Automatistes. The implication was an aesthetic related to stream-of-consciousness literature. Marxism and psychoanalysis, the prevailing intellectual mythologies of the day, were important elements in the automatiste cocktail, which, it need hardly be said, met with little encouragement from the church. The definitive manifesto of the group was the Refus Global, with the central essay by Borduas.

Automatism led to another reaction, by Les Plasticiens, who were more interested in colour and form than spontaneous expression. Charles Gagnon (a photographer and filmmaker as well), Yves Gaucher, Jacques Hurtubise, Guido Molinari and Claude Toussignant were some of the big names. Jean McEwen was president in the early 1960s of the Non-Figurative Artists Association of Montreal, a clearing house for the Plasticiens and their sympathizers.

If hard abstraction in turn fell in the 1980s to the more conceptual and political styles encompassed by such protean expressions as minimalism and postmodernism, it at least left Montreal secure as a place where it was possible to be many things other than boring. Some artists never signed up anywhere. "I never felt part of it," the anglo Montrealer Betty Goodwin said about the Borduas gang – even though she was as vigorously expressive as they of the inner consciousness. A Goodwin work of 1999 hung in the Cosmos show at the Montreal Museum of Fine Arts, an institution once scorned by the modernists.

In one of his many star turns on both stage and screen, the great Jean Duceppe played Maurice Duplessis in a 1972 production of the Quebec stage smash, Charbonneau et le chef, about the historic split between church and state in Quebec during the 1949 Asbestos strike. (Gazette file – Montreal Star)

Martha Allan's Montreal Repertory Theatre, which opened in 1930, produced shows in English and French. Montreal stage legends such as Gratien Gélinas and Christopher Plummer, here with young Mayor Jean Drapeau in 1956, honed their skills at the MRT. (GAZETTE FILES)

Montreal is at its best when its cultural components combine to produce something greater than the sum of its parts. A classic example was the collaboration between Quebec's leading playwright of the century, Michel Tremblay, and Dora Wasserman, founder and director of the Montreal Yiddish Theatre and tireless promoter of Jewish cultural theatre. Tremblay's work focuses on everyday life in Montreal's gritty neighbourhoods, and on this 1991 occasion, he worked with Wasserman on a Yiddish version of the first of his many hits, Les belles soeurs. (GAZETTE – MARIE FRANCE COALLIER)

For most of the last three decades, the English thespian torch has been carried by the Centaur Theatre. In this 1997 photo, the Centaur's longtime artistic director, Maurice Podbrey, charms Cultural Affairs Minister Louise Beaudoin as Podbrey's successor, Gordon McCall, looks on. Podbrey was one of the Centaur's founders in 1969 and remained the artistic director until his retirement in 1997. Among other things, he was instrumental in introducing the work of South African playwright Athol Fugard to North American audiences. (GAZETTE – JOHN KENNEY)

Dance is the art form in which the immigrant experience, in Montreal, has proven most decisive. Godmother of the genre was Ludmilla Chiriaeff, a Russian ballerina raised in Berlin, whose European roots were no impediment to the incorporation of Canadian motifs and the new technology of television into her vision of the discipline. No mere duster-off of classics, Les Grands Ballets Canadiens, founded by Chiriaeff in 1958, was open to short original works and even, in 1970, a choreographed version of the so-called rock opera Tommy. Apart from creating about 300 ballets, Chiriaeff established much of the Montreal infrastructure of ballet training. After a decade of direction by the American Lawrence Rhodes, who stressed collaborations with international choreographers, Les Grands continues to stage a satisfying balance of contemporary works and classics at Place des Arts.

Thanks in part to the Chiriaeff approach, Montreal has flourished as a centre for modern dance. Les Ballets Jazz de Montréal, founded in 1972 by Eddie Toussaint, the Hungarian ballerina Eva Von Genscy, and Geneviève Salbaing, nurtured a wildly popular blend of New-York-based Luigi hip swings and basic ballet technique – which in turn prompted the opening of ballet-jazz schools across the country. Toussaint, a Haitian immigrant, moved on to cross-pollinate foreign and domestic influences in his own populist company, Ballet de Montréal.

Over the last 15 years, the Montreal scene has been dominated by more experimental outfits: La La La Human Steps, under Edouard Lock; O Vertigo, directed by Ginette Laurin; and Montréal Danse, founded by Paul-André Fortier with expat American Daniel Jackson and now led by another American, Kathy Casey. Of course, there is a festival: the Festival International de Nouvelle Danse. Some would contend that by the late 1990s the Montreal dance scene had been drawn too far into the

realm of "new dance" – with pretensions to social commentary functioning as ballast for technically undistinguished performance. Sometimes the postmodern devolves into the post-pornographic, with no small interest from the media. Whatever her other talents, Quebec City-born Marie Chouinard will forever be remembered for urinating on stage. Still, the sheer volume of footwork – good, bad or indifferent – guarantees Montreal a place on the global dance map.

Theatre, obviously, is rigorously defined by language. In Montreal, religion has been equally decisive, as Roman Catholic abhorrence of the stage delayed the development of serious French-language theatre until the middle of the century. English theatre emerged earlier through the Montreal Repertory Theatre, established by Martha Allan, the lone surviving child of financier Sir Hugh Allan. Apart from cultivating such future celebrities as Christopher Plummer, this amateur troupe of high aims created a spiritual precedent for the professional English-language Centaur Theatre, founded in 1969 by South African Maurice Podbrey. The Centaur has staged contemporary international drama without ignoring the possibilities of Montreal playwrights, such as David Fennario, whose bilingual Balconville was the company's most famous contribution to Canadian social realism.

The MRT also engaged Gratien Gélinas, who dominated what worthwhile French theatre there was in the 1930s with his satirical sketches and the seminal 1948 down-and-out epic, Tit-Coq. While this play was blazing a trail for modern drama in Quebec, Jean Gascon and Jean-Louis Roux established a great classical house, the Théâtre du Nouveau Monde, in 1951. After the Théâtre de Quat'Sous and the Théâtre du Rideau Vert opened their doors, Montreal looked suspiciously a centre for French theatre.

Rideau Vert made history in 1968 by staging Michel Tremblay's Les Belles-Soeurs, a not-

Mid-century movements for social democracy and civil rights were championed in Montreal by people like lawyer, professor and poet Frank Scott (centre). Scott, along with Irving Layton (left) and Louis Dudek, were outstanding poets who greatly illuminated Montreal's literary scene this century. All three were grand old men of Canadian letters when this photo was taken in 1983. (GAZETTE – TEDD CHURCH)

too-nostalgic portrait, in ear-numbing joual, of the women who populated the playwright's own working-class neighbourhood. Realism has given way lately to experimentalism: Carbone 14 and Théâtre UBU, both with European connections, are two of the more durable off-off companies and the Festival de Théâtre des Amériques guarantees stimulation. René-Daniel Dubois is notable among the aggressive deconstructionists, writing plays that often involve the author in multiple roles (not to mention sexual identities). Among directors, Robert Lepage, in demand around the world, represents the summit of the contemporary sensibility and technical virtuosity that characterize theatre in Montreal. Yet amid all the progressivism, the Théâtre Jean Duceppe, in Place des Arts, stages middle-of-the-road repertoire for

appreciative crowds. Musicals have always done well in Montreal – ask impresario Sam Gesser. And the city's many communities have often found theatrical expression, whether in the realist dramas of Italian-Canadian Vittorio Rossi or in the Montreal Yiddish Theatre, upholding the legacy of what was once Montreal's third-most-spoken language.

It was natural for the city of languages to sprout literature. In the 1920s, a McGill Group of poets (F.R. Scott, A.J.M. Smith, A.M. Klein), with handy outlets in the McGill Daily and the McGill Fortnightly Review, attempted to purge their work of Victorian lavender and produce a modernism combining social awareness with a feeling for Canadian landscape. Twenty years later, the Northern Review, edited by John Sutherland, led the way, bringing together Scott

Stephen Leacock's day job was as a professor of economics at McGill University, but he is best remembered for his sideline as a writer of deathless humour with a distinctly Canadian flavour. His Can-Lit classic, Sunshine Sketches of a Little Town, *was first serialized in The Montreal Star in 1912.* (GAZETTE FILES – MONTREAL STAR)

Canadian literary icon Gabrielle Roy came from Manitoba but spent some of her most productive years in Montreal. She worked as a freelance journalist, and in 1945 published Bonheur d'occasion, *her most famous novel, set in the city's hardscrabble St. Henri district.* (MONTREAL STAR)

and the poets Louis Dudek and Irving Layton. The latter became famous for his anti-establishment posturing and free-love polemics – so much so, that he is seldom now given credit for the technical mastery of his best verse.

If Layton was the most flamboyant exponent of anglo Montreal poetry, Leonard Cohen achieved the widest popularity, with lyrics steeped in the pathos of failed romance and the imagery of his home town (which he frequented along with Greece, New York and California). His work as a novelist and singer-songwriter was comparably appealing. The premier novelist of Montreal is Mordecai Richler, who has documented the Jewish experience with vividness and (unlike his predecessor Klein) a mordant spirit that occasionally earned him accusations of anti-Semitism. Richler is viewed most

antagonistically, however, by francophone intellectuals who resent his exposure of the absurdities of separatist doctrine, epitomized by a New Yorker article of 1991.

Of the same generation is Mavis Gallant, a resident of Paris since the 1950s who nevertheless treats Canadian themes in her short stories. Before Richler came Hugh MacLennan, a Nova Scotian who settled in Montreal in 1935 to teach Latin at Lower Canada College. A nationalist who treated Canada as a country worth writing about on an epic scale, MacLennan created, with his novel *Two Solitudes*, an enduring image of our cultural chasm. His last novel, *Voices in Time*, was set in Montreal 50 years after a nuclear holocaust. While Stephen Leacock immortalized the fictional Ontario town of Mariposa in his humorous literature, this

Montreal novelist Mordecai Richler put his home town and the vibrant St. Urbain Street neighbourhood of his adolescence on the world literary map in a succession of best-selling novels such as The Apprenticeship of Duddy Kravitz, Joshua Then and Now *and, most recently,* Barney's Version. *He also became a bête noire in Quebec nationalist circles for his denunciations of Quebec anti-Semitism and satirization of Quebec's language laws in the international press. Here he is right, at a 1976 election rally in support of Nick Auf der Maur of the short-lived Democratic Alliance party. At left is former Montreal executive committee chairman Michael Fainstat.* (GAZETTE – MICHAEL DUGAS)

economics professor spent most of his daily life at McGill and the University Club, which he helped found.

Belfast-born Brian Moore needs to be mentioned as an international author who wrote about Montreal, where he lived for 10 years until 1959. Saul Bellow, born in Lachine in 1915, became famous for books such as *Herzog*. He won the Nobel Prize for literature in 1976. In the 1990s – despite the vaunted anglo attri-

tion – Trevor Ferguson, born in Montreal, was producing respected novels and assaulting the best-seller list with a detective thriller, *City of Ice*, set in Montreal.

Canadian novels in French, though not as dominated as one might expect by Montreal-born authors, often adopt the vibrant metropolis as their setting. Gabrielle Roy, a bilingual Manitoban, wrote about working-class Montrealers in perhaps the most famous of all French-Canadian novels: *Bonheur d'occasion*, translated as *The Tin Flute*. Marie-Claire Blais and the prolific Yves Thériault were born in Quebec City but ended up in Montreal. Roch Carrier, perhaps stimulated by negative example, has written nostalgically about rural Quebec from the vantage of the city.

Film has blossomed somewhat late in Montreal, given the popularity of the Montreal World Film Festival, which is dedicated, unlike its glitzy Toronto counterpart, to international art cinema. The National Film Board attracted some ambitious francophone directors in the 1950s, but the breakthrough in Quebec came in 1971 with *Mon Oncle Antoine* by Montreal-born Claude Jutra. Denys Arcand became an international figure in the 1980s, winning awards in Cannes with both *Le Déclin de l'Empire Américain* (which did for the Outremont intelligentsia what Fellini did for the corrupt elite of Rome) and the powerful allegory *Jésus de Montréal*. Jean-Claude Lauzon, before his death in 1997, attracted attention with his shocking images. Norman McLaren was a world leader in film animation. The continued popularity of Montreal as a backdrop for American movies (St. Jacques Street made do for lower Broadway in a 1999 film about P.T. Barnum) and the blossoming of the city's film-technology industry guarantee the city a robust future in the film business.

Perhaps the future of the arts in Montreal is threatened by its very fecundity. The list of

Claude Jutra's Mon Oncle Antoine *put Quebec film-making on the map.* (G<small>AZETTE FILES</small>)

recipients of Montreal Urban Community grants in 1999 included a ridiculous 40 theatre companies. Numbers in other sectors were comparably prodigious. The financial problems that torment the Montreal Symphony Orchestra have a lot to do with the local oversupply of music, much of which is offered cheap or free. Yet to those who rightly equate activity in the arts with the spirit and enterprise of a city, Montreal is likely to remain – however our forebears might disapprove – an intoxicating place to live. ◆

Director Denys Arcand, shown here with members of his production team, gained international acclaim for provocative French-language films such as Le déclin de l'empire américain *and* Jésus de Montréal. (G<small>AZETTE</small> – L<small>EN</small> S<small>IDAWAY</small>)

Ups and downs
and other milestones

BY JOHN **KALBFLEISH**

L ET US PAUSE A MOMENT for the sake of Arthur Lenoir. Precious few others, we can be sure, have spared him a thought for 100 years now.

Lenoir was a shunter for the Grand Trunk Railway in Montreal. It was the last Saturday of the year – indeed, of the century – and he was coupling some cars in the Bonaventure Station railyard, near where the Montreal Planetarium now stands. It was icy, with snow lying about, and somehow he slipped. As The Gazette laconically reported afterward, "his head, coming

It was a Quebec tradition in the early century to build elaborate triumphal arches for monumental occasions, such as this one erected at the corner of Cherrier and St. Hubert for the 1910 Eucharistic Congress, when the eyes of the Roman Catholic world were on Montreal. The six-day international gathering of Catholic clergy and laity was the first held in the Americas. Written on the arch, which was dismantled after the festivities, is: "Come unto me and I will give you rest." (ARCHIVES - ROMAN CATHOLIC ARCHDIOCESE OF MONTREAL)

PREVIOUS PAGES

Here's to you, Montreal! A shower of radiance lights up the night sky over the festive city and the Jacques Cartier Bridge during a 1996 fireworks display. (GAZETTE - PIERRE OBENDRAUF)

One of the Expo site's most prominent landmarks was the U.S. pavilion, a giant geodesic dome designed by the visionary Buckminster Fuller, was reduced to a charred skeleton in 1976 when a spark from a welder's torch touched off a spectacular conflagration that consumed the structure's plastic covering. It has since been reborn as the Biosphere, and is once again a Montreal attraction. (GAZETTE FILES)

between the bunters, was so badly crushed that the unfortunate fellow survived but a few minutes."

The grisly demise of Arthur Lenoir was reported in The Gazette on Monday, January 1, 1900. The death of this otherwise unknown Montrealer was the first the newspaper would record in the 20th century (though The Gazette, as was the custom then, would not acknowledge the fin de siècle until the end of 1900). But beyond that brief news item, there was barely a ripple as the waters of history closed quickly over Lenoir. So it is with people, no less in Montreal than anywhere else.

Tragedy alternates with our triumphs, sadness with our joy. Indeed, there are surely still among us a few Montrealers who have witnessed each of the grand, public high and low points that this century has visited on the city.

One of the grandest of the century's events in Montreal is today almost completely forgotten. Yet, for a glorious week in September 1910, the eyes of Roman Catholics around the world were riveted on the city. Montreal was to see nothing like it for another 74 years and the arrival of Pope John Paul II, and even at that the papal visit arguably must stand in second place.

The occasion was the 21st International Eucharistic Congress, a six-day gathering of clergy and laity bound on reconfirming their devotion to the solemn rite of communion, the eucharist, in which the suffering and death of Jesus are commemorated. The congress was being held for the first time in the western hemisphere, and Pope Pius X sent Cardinal Vicenzo Vannutelli as his legate. On the final day of the congress, under cloudless blue skies, an estimated 50,000 people paraded through the streets of Montreal. There were bands, police and firemen, soldiers, members of parish societies including Mohawks from Kahnawake and Chinese Catholics "proudly flying the dragon banner of the Celestial Kingdom," Trappists and Jesuits, priests and bishops, a children's choir,

The street procession on the final day of the 1910 Eucharistic Congress took more than four hours to pass. It wound up at Fletcher's Field (now Jeanne Mance Park) where a congregation of half a million assembled for a service of benediction, the largest gathering of any sort in Canadian history to that point. (ARCHIVES - ROMAN CATHOLIC ARCHDIOCESE OF MONTREAL)

zouaves, Prime Minister Wilfrid Laurier and Premier Lomer Gouin. Cardinal Vannutelli appeared near the end of the solemn procession holding aloft a golden monstrance containing the consecrated host.

The parade took more than four hours to pass. It made its way to Fletcher's Field, today's Jeanne Mance Park, where a service of benediction was held. It is thought that half a million people were there, and if so, the number exceeded the 350,000 who attended the papal mass at Jarry Park in 1984. It was, as The Gazette rather breathlessly reported, "the greatest demonstration of any kind – historical, religious or political – which Canada has ever witnessed."

The end of that decade in Montreal was marked with processions of a less joyous sort.

Funerals. The Spanish flu epidemic that raged around the world in 1918 and 1919 did not spare Montreal. In October 1918 alone, there were 10,201 cases of the disease in the city, 1,706 of them fatal. Public events everywhere were canceled. For example, fears of contagion ensured that the Oct. 21 opening of the Mount Royal railway tunnel from what's now Central Station was greeted not by speeches, but by an utter absence of ceremony.

Day after day, solemn funeral processions made their way to Montreal's cemeteries. At the height of the epidemic, a special streetcar, normally used to carry a single coffin to the Hawthorndale cemetery at the east end of Montreal Island, handled nine or 10 stacked on top of one another. At Mount Royal Cemetery,

John Paul II was the first pope to visit Montreal. (GAZETTE FILES)

gravediggers had to be paid an extra dollar a day to stay on the job. Many years later, a nun living in retirement in Outremont would recollect from her childhood perhaps the most poignant sort of procession of them all: "Well do I recall watching from my window the many hearses coming up the hill on their way to the cemetery. Of special concern were the little white hearses carrying the bodies of babies. We used to count these, for they made a particular impression on us as children."

Less than a decade later, another tragedy struck Montreal. Children were the victims of the Laurier Palace fire of Jan. 9, 1927. Considering the number who died – 78 – and the awful suddenness with which their lives were snuffed out, it was the greatest single disaster in Montreal this century.

It was a Sunday afternoon, and about 900 youngsters, some as young as 4, were crammed into the cinema on Ste. Catherine Street East. It was a disaster waiting to happen. Many of the children crowded the aisles, for the Laurier Palace had seats for just 786. The pair of narrow stairways that connected the balcony with the ground floor were narrow and dark and, as was later to become clear, the exit doors from the building did not work properly.

On the screen that day was Toronto-born Mary Pickford, starring in a comedy called *Get 'em Young*. The house lights had been down for about 10 minutes when someone noticed smoke. Flames appeared; the children panicked. Those in the balcony rushed to get out, and in one of the unlit stairwells, apparently just five steps from safety, someone fell. Others pushing from behind tumbled on top. In the horror that followed, few burned to death. Most died either from asphyxiation or from being crushed. A few children were pulled alive from the smoldering building, only to expire moments later in the street. An off-duty policeman, Albert Boisseau, showed up to give his colleagues a hand and discovered that all three of his children were among the victims.

The decades wore on; memories faded. By the 1940s, very few among Montreal children would have understood why they could not go to the movies like children elsewhere. The reason was simple. The year after the Laurier Palace fire, the provincial legislature toughened the law to prohibit anyone under the age of 16 from entering a cinema. The law would not be scrapped until 1967, when the world came to Montreal for Expo.

As great an outburst of spontaneous joy as Montreal has ever seen exploded on May 7, 1945, when Nazi Germany finally surrendered. Word came about 9:30 in the morning, and by 11 the downtown streets were jammed with men, women and children laughing, shouting, hugging and kissing. Many streetcars couldn't move, especially around the corner of Peel and Ste. Catherine streets, which seemed to be the focus of the delirium. Sirens, car horns and ships'

The Laurier Palace theatre was gutted by a 1927 fire in which 78 people, most of them children, some as young as 4, died at a Saturday matinee. (GAZETTE FILES)

whistles in the harbour added to the din. Flags of many nations, but especially the Red Ensign and the Union Jack, appeared like magic in windows and on hastily erected staffs, and paper rained down from office buildings on the streets below. The normally staid canyon of St. James Street, still the financial heart of Canada, was especially boisterous as cars with celebrants balanced precariously on their running boards careered along its length. Most enterprises shut their doors – bars and liquor outlets by provincial fiat – or went through the motions of business with the most skeletal staffs. Yet it was not all triumph; joy was tempered with sadness. On that day, an RCMP constable in Montreal named Coutlee received word that his son had been killed in service overseas. People could be seen forsaking the revelry and trickling all day into the city's churches to give thanks for the war's end or perhaps to mourn the loss of a relative or friend. One woman was on her knees praying in front of the cenotaph in Dominion Square, now Place du Canada. And what must we make of the "white-haired man" who The Gazette's reporter saw in tears at Papineau

Avenue and Craig Street, or the girl who "wept unashamedly on a balcony on Amherst Street just above Sherbrooke" – were they tears of joy or in fact of grief?

To be sure, Montreal that day was not unusual; it was much the same throughout the Allied nations. But the triumph to be ours in 1967 was unique. That was the time of Expo 67, and though the great world's exhibition stretched from April to the end of October, each day seemed like part of an endless summer. More than 50 million visitors, twice the number anticipated, were drawn from around the world to see the city and help celebrate Canada's centennial. And, oh, how they were dazzled: by Expo's national days with their performers and exotic cuisines, by the audacity of Moshe Safdie's Habitat, by a monorail, by split-screen film techniques, by the huge American and Soviet pavilions warily eyeing each other while the rest of us wandered back and forth sampling their delights, by the carefree joys of La Ronde late into the night.

Montreal was on a roll. The métro had just opened, and new expressways were snaking

The range of emotions at the homecoming to Montreal of Canadian troops after World War II shows in these 1945 photos. Joseph Boissoneault of Danville, Que., (left) looks through tears of joy at his returning son, Rifleman Adrien Boissoneault, a veteran of the Hong Kong siege. Capt. Stanley Banfill (above) who served in Hong Kong saw his 4-year-old son Martin for the first time upon his return home. A wounded Pte. H.W. Dickson (bottom left) of the Lorne Scots was reunited with his wife and they went home to Hutchison Street. (GAZETTE FILES)

around and through the city. New buildings like Place Ville Marie and Place Bonaventure were transforming the heart of downtown. Two years later, major league baseball in the shape of the fittingly named Expos arrived.

But Expo spoiled us. We came to believe that things could only get better. The 1976 Olympics proved how wrong we could be. Yes, the world once again came calling – though minus Taiwan, miffed that the People's Republic got to call itself China, and 30 nations in Africa, Latin America and the Middle East, protesting against a New Zealand rugby tour of South Africa. Yes, the stadium was a technological and aesthetic marvel – if you could overlook our inability to finish it on time. And yes, to this day, the wonderful performances by the likes of Nadia Comaneci are the stuff of dreams – even if the Games' billion-dollar cost overrun remains a nightmare.

A giant portrait of Chinese leader Chiang Kai-Shek – who would soon be overthrown by Mao Tse Tung – was drawn through the streets of Chinatown in a parade celebrating the World War II allied victory in the Pacific, in August 1945. Note the equal billing for U.S. president Harry Truman (right foreground) and Soviet dictator Joseph Stalin (left) in the pre-Cold War order. (Gazette files - Montreal Star)

The slaughter at the École Polytechnique on December 6, 1989, was perhaps Montreal's most horrifying low point of the century. Marc Lépine, 25, went to the Université de Montréal's engineering school with a semi-automatic rifle. Women were his target: he murdered 14 and wounded nine others, plus four men, before turning his weapon on himself. On his body was found a rambling diatribe against women who dared to seek equality, plus a hit list of 15 prominent Quebec women including a provincial cabinet minister, a labour leader and several media figures.

The images of that dreadful episode remain part of Montrealers' common currency: Montreal police officer Pierre Leclair rushing to the scene to help deal with the carnage, only to discover that his daughter, Maryse, was one of those slain (a haunting echo of what befell Constable Boisseau 62 years before at the Laurier Palace), the mocking contrast of beau-

tiful white snowflakes drifting gently down while the dead and wounded were wheeled from the school, the white coffins row on row at the funeral in Notre Dame Basilica five days later. The city – indeed, the whole country – was united in horror and grief.

It was adversity that united Montrealers, as well as people living in a broad swath from Georgian Bay to Granby in the Townships, to the Maritimes, and through the northeastern United States, in January 1998 when the ice storm of the century struck. The numbers are still chilling: half the population of Quebec lost power, in some cases for as long as 33 days; thousands of power poles, transformers and other installations were destroyed; trees were devastated; damage exceeded $1.1 billion, including insurance claims of $871 million in Quebec; and more than 20 people died in the greater Montreal area. Yet through it all, people stuck together.

Montreal's signal triumph this century was Expo 67, the dazzling world's fair the city hosted as the showcase of Canada's centennial year. More than 50 million thronged to the fair, double the number expected. The Expo magic was such that few quibbled about the half billion dollars it went over budget. Expo's pavilions were a symphony of the architectural avant garde, as in this view (left) of the Canadian pavilion. From kings and queens and presidents to babes in arms (right), everyone had their Expo passport. Expo was a triumph for its prime mover, Jean Drapeau, and for others, as this photo by Gordon Beck below suggests, a marvelous place to visit.

It was Canada's most horrifying massacre of the century. A lone gunman named Marc Lépine singled out women in his December 1989 killing rampage at the École Polytechnique. He killed 14 before he killed himself. A memorial to the slain students was erected in 1991. In this photo, (above) Serge Marsolais placed flowers at the unveiling. The image of snow falling as ambulance technicians rushed victims from the building is one Montrealers will remember for a long time. (GAZETTE FILES)

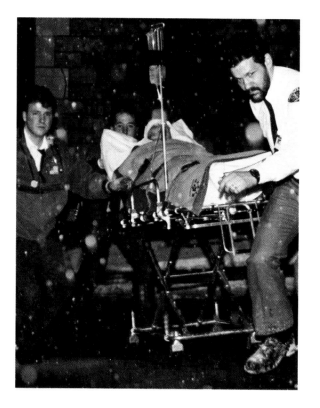

Montrealers who had power were quick to open their homes to their less fortunate neighbours. Police, firemen and volunteers went door to door checking for people or pets in need of help. Ice-storm anecdotes are beyond counting, but time and again they return to the theme of people helping one another.

Now, at the end of this tumultuous century of many high points and lows, Montreal is enjoying another high point in its progression. Every year, Montrealers and visitors come together in a series of festivals that make the city, once the snow disappears, an incomparable magnet for bons vivants. Few other cities can match the succession of the Jazz Festival, FrancoFolies, the fireworks competition, the Juste Pour Rire / Just for Laughs laughathon, Nuits d'Afrique, the Fringe Festival, tam-tams on Mount Royal,

Like the skeleton of a prehistoric monster, the Olympic Stadium's supporting beams loom over the construction site in this 1975 photo. Montrealers will be paying off the stadium's monstrous cost overrun well into the new century. (GAZETTE – MICHAEL DUGAS)

The great ice storm of 1998 was one of Montreal's worst natural calamities of the century. But it was also an occasion for Montrealers to reaffirm their city's undying spirit. Here an NDG resident tries to figure out the best way around a fallen tree blocking Oxford Avenue. (Gazette – Peter Martin)

the Montreal Grand Prix, Carifiesta, the International Film Festival, the Fêtes Gourmandes Internationales on Île Notre Dame, the Tour de l'Île, powwows at Kanesatake and Kahnawake and the back-to-back St. Jean Baptiste and Canada Day celebrations.

We began our survey of Montreal highpoints and lows with the death of Arthur Lenoir. Let us end with the greatest triumph of all, a birth. We hear a lot about how couples have been engaged in elaborate contortions to ensure their expected child is born in the first moment of the new millennium. An auspicious debut, to be sure: but let us also consider what will be

Montreal's last births of the 1900s. These children will have the potential to make their mark on a great city and to share in delights and, it must be said, sorrows that we can scarcely imagine of the 21st century. ◆

1900

✳ Like many other years of the 20th century, hockey and politics dominated the news in Montreal in 1900. A three-day riot erupted in February when McGill University students, celebrating a British battle victory during the South African Boer war, clashed with francophone students. The French Canadians were protesting against Canadian involvement in Britain's imperial wars.

✳ In March, the Montreal Shamrocks won hockey's Stanley Cup, defeating the Winnipeg Victorias, two games to one, before a home crowd. It was the second year in a row the Shamrocks had won the Cup, which had been donated by Governor-General Lord Stanley in 1893 for the amateur hockey champions of Canada.

1901

✳ In August, an 11-week strike at Canadian Pacific Railway in Montreal ended when the company agreed to recognize the trainmen's brotherhood as the workers' official representative. Wages were not raised and the contract applied only to foremen and workers with at least one year's service.

1904

✳ The exclusive Mount Royal Club, at Stanley and Sherbrooke streets, was destroyed in January by a fire in which a fireman and the club's night guard were killed. The club, founded in 1899, was a favourite haunt of English Montreal's wealthy merchants and financiers. It re-opened two years later.

Archbishop Paul Bruchési ushered the city's Catholic flock into the 20th century. (GAZETTE FILES)

1906

✳ Montreal recorded its first auto fatality. Antoine Toutant, 47, a resident of Poupart Street, was killed on Ste. Catherine Street when struck by a car driven by Thomas Atkinson. By the end of the century, about 90 people a year were killed on Montreal roads.

✳ Sunday activities in the city were severely curtailed following a temperance crusade by Archbishop Paul Bruchési, who called for an end to political meetings, theatrical performances and dances on the Lord's Day. The following year, the archbishop urged Montreal Catholics to stay away from the cinema on Sundays.

1907

✳ McGill University opened its Macdonald College agricultural facility in Ste. Anne de Bellevue. It was named for tobacco industrialist and philanthropist Sir William Macdonald, who donated over $11 million to McGill.

1908

✳ Ernest Rutherford was awarded the Nobel Prize in chemistry for research he conducted at McGill University into radioactivity. After he returned to England, Rutherford went on to make another fundamental discovery: the nucleus of the atom. McGill's physics building is named after him.

1909

✳ The Montreal Canadiens hockey club was founded. The team went on to win 24 Stanley Cups, the first in 1916, one year before the creation of the National Hockey League, and the last of the centu-

The Montreal Canadiens hockey club was founded in 1909 and went on to win the Stanley Cup 24 times during the century. This team photo dates back to the 1940s! (Gazette files)

ry in 1993. The team won more Stanley Cup championships than any other team in the NHL.

1 9 1 0

✳ On January 10, the newspaper Le Devoir was first published. It was the political platform of founder and nationalist leader Henri Bourassa, a proponent of French minority rights and provincial autonomy.

✳ The first bachelor of arts degree awarded to a woman by a French-language university in Quebec was granted by the Université de Montréal. It came more than two decades after women began graduating from McGill University.

1 9 1 2

✳ The maiden voyage of the supposedly unsinkable Titanic ended in tragedy when it hit an iceberg and sank. Some 1,500 passengers and crew were lost. About 32 passengers had Montreal as their destination; 20 of them drowned, including Harry Markland Molson, of the banking and brewing family, and Charles Melville Hays, president of the Grand Trunk Railway.

✳ Carrie M. Derick became the first woman university professor in Canada. She was named professor of morphological botany at McGill University. Derick also was an active suffragette and the first president of the Société du Suffrage Féminin in 1912.

✳ In July, construction began on a 4.8-kilometre tunnel through Mount Royal, to connect the northern suburbs of the city with the downtown area. The first passenger train passed through the tunnel in 1918. The opening ceremony, however, was curtailed because of the influenza epidemic in the city at that time.

✳ Louis Cyr, Montreal strongman, died.

Brother André, one of Montreal's most venerable figures of the century, believed to have miraculous healing powers. He built a wooden shrine on the slope of Mount Royal in 1904 that drew thousands of pilgrims and inspired the construction of St. Joseph's Oratory. (Gazette files)

1914

✻ The cornerstone for the Sun Life Assurance building was laid by company president Robertson Macaulay. With 26 storeys, it was the tallest office building in the British Empire for decades. Sun Life moved its head office out of Montreal in 1979.

✻ In August, crowds filled Montreal streets as war between Britain and Germany was declared. The newly formed Princess Patricia's Canadian Light Infantry sailed from Montreal August 29.

1916

✻ The stone crypt of what was to become St. Joseph's Oratory was begun, with the Oratory finally being officially inaugurated in 1955. The church was the outcome of a wooden shrine built in 1904 by Brother André, a novitiate and doorkeeper in the Congregation of the Holy Cross. He was believed to have miraculous powers. Brother André died in 1937, at 91, and was beatified in 1982. An estimated 18,000 people attended his funeral.

1917

✻ The National Hockey League was formed in Montreal with the first NHL game played on December 19, 1917.

Gentle giant Louis Cyr's storied feats of strength made him to Quebecers what Paul Bunyan is to Americans. His statue on Place St. Henri stands as an inspiration to Montrealers of all ages. (GAZETTE – GORDON BECK)

Belmont Park was Montreal's playground for decades, and fountain of memories for youngsters. This is what the gateway looked like in the 1940s; all were welcome, save zoot-suiters. (GAZETTE FILES)

These little refuges, still seen in city squares and parks like Carré St. Louis and Cabot Park, were the creation of Camillien Houde. They were built as public toilets – part of Houde's public works programs to create jobs during the Depression – and styled after the vespasiennes in Paris, so named after Emperor Vespasian who had come up with the idea for ancient Rome. In Montreal, even though the word "vespasiennes" was engraved over the door, they became known as camilliennes after the mayor. (GAZETTE FILES)

Montreal's most colourful mayor of the century, Camillien Houde. (GAZETTE FILES)

1918

✻ On April 1, an unruly crowd protesting the passage of the federal Military Services Act tried to capture the city armoury. Ottawa declared martial law and troops were called in to control rioters.
✻ Later that year, the Spanish flu plagued the city, killing 1,706 by the end of October.
✻ On November 11, Montrealers cheered as the cessation of fighting in Europe was announced. Armistice was celebrated in the streets by thousands.

1919

✻ The Canadian Jewish Congress was founded in Montreal with 209 delegates attending from across Canada.

1923

✻ Belmont Park in Cartierville opened. More than half a million Montrealers flocked to the amusement park every summer from the time it opened in 1923 until it closed 60 years later.

1924

✻ On November 29, 8,000 hockey fans flocked to the newly opened Forum, where the Canadiens beat the Toronto St. Patricks 7-1.
✻ On Christmas Eve, the illuminated cross on Mount Royal, commissioned by the Société St. Jean Baptiste, was lit for the first time. It stands where a wooden cross was thought to have been erected by Jacques Cartier in 1535. It was designed by Rev. Pierre Dupainges and lit by 156 bulbs. Now the cross is operated by a fibreoptic system.

1926

✻ Montreal's city hall opened on February 15. The building was a reconstruction of a building gutted by fire in 1922.

1927

✻ On January 9, one of Montreal's worst disasters occurred when a fire broke out at the Laurier Palace

Mayor Camillien Houde significantly altered the face of Montreal with massive public-works programs that nearly bankrupted the city. Many of Montreal's parks, playgrounds, tunnels, police and fire stations, the Botanical Garden, the chalet at the Mount Royal lookout (shown here around 1935), and farmers' markets including Jean Talon and Atwater were built during Houde's reign. (GAZETTE FILES)

theatre during an afternoon movie. Seventy-eight children died in the resulting stampede.

1928

✳ Montrealers elected Camillien Houde, then 39, as their mayor. It was his first of seven mayoralty election victories. He remained in office until 1954, except for brief intervals including a period of internment (1940-44) for urging Montrealers not to register for military service.

1930

✳ The Great Depression hit Montreal hard, with bread lines forming and soup kitchens opening to feed the jobless. By 1934, at the height of the Depression, one-quarter of the city's inhabitants depended on some sort of government financial assistance.

✳ On May 24, the Jacques Cartier Bridge opened, joining Montreal to the south shore of the St. Lawrence River. Originally called the Montreal Harbour Bridge, it was renamed in 1934. It took four years to build, at a cost of $18 million.

1931

✳ On June 17, the 3,700-ton oil tanker Cymbeline exploded at the Canadian Vickers shipbuilding plant and 27 people, including four firemen, were killed.

✳ On November. 1, André Laurendeau, in a manifesto aimed at young French Canadians, urged them to "reject their proletarian status and seize their fair share of economic power in Quebec and Canada". Published in the Université de Montréal student newspaper, the article called for action against "foreign capitalists" who kept French Canadians in servile roles.

Lionel Groulx (GAZETTE FILES)

✳ After much lobbying by women, Quebec finally forced the provincial bar association to admit women as lawyers and changed the laws that severely restricted women's property and legal rights. Despite those hard-won advances, Quebec women's legal status was similar to that of minors.

1 9 3 3

✳ The Mount Royal chalet, commissioned by Mayor Camillien Houde as a Depression project in 1930, officially opened with a dance held by Kiwanis International.

✳ On September 20, a newly formed organization called the Fascist Party of Canada claimed 25,000 members. Anaclet Chalifoux, former leader of the Federation of Labour Clubs of Quebec, was one of the founders.

1 9 3 4

✳ Abbé Lionel Groulx argued in an article that French Canadians required a forceful leader to restore pride. Groulx, a teacher at Collège Ste. Marie, cited Italy's Benito Mussolini as an example of the kind of leader needed.

✳ In November, the Société des Concerts Symphoniques de Montreal was founded. In 1953, it became the Montreal Symphony Orchestra.

✳ In December, 61 Canadians, including four Bronfman brothers, were charged by the RCMP with evasion of payment of $5 million of customs duties on liquor allegedly smuggled into the United States during that country's Prohibition era. The next year, the case went to trial but was thrown out by the judge in June.

✳ Dr. Wilder Penfield, a neurosurgeon at the Royal Victoria Hospital, founded the Montreal Neurological Institute. It rapidly became an international centre for teaching, research and treatment of diseases related to the brain. Penfield's work and research as a scientist won him international acclaim.

1 9 3 7

✳ The Padlock Law was introduced in the National Assembly, allowing authorities to close educational, religious or community organizations suspected

Dr. Norman Bethune practiced in Montreal for a time before he became a hero of the communist revolution in China, where he is pictured in 1938. (GAZETTE FILES)

One of the century's great men of science was Dr. Wilder Penfield, a Montrealer world renowned for his breakthrough achievements in neuromedicine. (GAZETTE FILES – MONTREAL STANDARD)

of teaching or advocating communism or anti-religious views.

✱ On March 8, Montreal Canadiens hockey hero Howie Morenz died of an injury suffered in a game six weeks previously. He was named to the Hockey Hall of Fame in 1945.

✱ On June 17, Norman Bethune, a Montreal doctor and public health-care advocate who joined the Spanish Civil War, was greeted by a cheering crowd on his return to the city. While in Spain, he was credited with organizing the first mobile blood transfusion unit. Bethune later went to China, where he served Communist forces resisting Japanese invaders. He died there of blood poisoning in 1939.

1939

✱ On July 23, a mass wedding was held in De Lorimier Stadium to marry 105 couples as 25,000 people looked on. The ceremony was planned by a local youth organization and 105 priests officiated, along with Archbishop Georges Gauthier.

✱ Montrealers filled the streets as news of war between Britain and Germany was announced.

1940

✱ Quebec women were granted the right to vote in provincial elections, almost 22 years after they were awarded voting rights in federal elections.

✱ On August 5, Montreal Mayor Camillien Houde was arrested under the War Measures Act and interned in a camp outside Montreal. He had publically protested registration for military service and called for defiance of the law. He was released in 1944 and re-elected as mayor.

1941

✱ The first tank manufactured in Canada rolled off an assembly line in Montreal.

✱ Émile Nelligan, whose sad and romantic poetry won him near legendary status in some Quebec literary circles, died at 61. Nelligan produced 170 poems, sonnets, songs and prose poems and spent most of his life in a psychiatric hospital.

✱ Hugh MacLennan, a Nova Scotian who had made Montreal his home as an English teacher, wrote his first novel, *Barometer Rising.* MacLennan went on to become one of Canada's finest novelists and the first major English-speaking Canadian to portray the country's national character. *Two Solitudes* was published in 1945, dealing with English-French tensions in Quebec. While writing, he taught English at McGill University from 1951 to 1981.

1942

✱ In Lafontaine Park, thousands of Montrealers turned out to praise 17 Dieppe heroes, five of whom were from Montreal. The ill-fated raid on the French town of Dieppe by about 5,000 Canadians was designed to test German coastal defences. More than 900 Canadians were killed and 1,874 taken prisoner.

1943

✱ On July 22, Trans-Canada Air Lines inaugurated the first regular transatlantic commercial flight from Montreal to Britain. The plane carried three passengers and mail, making the 4,800-kilometre flight in 12 hours and 25 minutes.

✱ Primary school attendance became compulsory in Quebec.

1944

✱ Sailors and zoot-suiters clashed in Montreal, with 42 arrests.

The Gazette.

MONTREAL, MONDAY, JULY 24, 1939.—TWENTY-TWO PAGES

PRICE FIVE CENTS

COUPLES WED SIMULTANEOUSLY IN STADIUM CEREMONY

25,000 LOOK ON AS 105 PRIESTS PERFORM RITE

Brides and Grooms, All of J.O.C., Keep Calm at Altar

THRONG DEEPLY STIRRED

No Untoward Incident Mars Brilliant Spectacle Despite Scorching Sun

SCENE AT STADIUM DURING MASS MARRIAGE CEREMONIES

SPAIN EXTENDS ARMY SHAKE-UP | 400 Taken Ill at J.O.C. Pageant As Result of Heat, Exhaustion | RIVER TRAGEDY PROBE AWAITED | U.K.-JAPAN DEAL DETAILS TODAY

Mass weddings were a pre-war phenomenon in Montreal. In this 1939 ceremony, 105 couples were wed simultaneously before a crowd of 25,000 at De Lorimier Stadium. Five years later, 98 of the couples gathered for an anniversary reunion on the grounds of St. Joseph's Oratory. (GAZETTE FILES)

✻ On April 25, a four-engine RAF Liberator bomber, bound for Europe from Dorval, crashed into six houses in Griffintown, killing the crew of five and 10 people on the ground.

1945

✻ Montrealers celebrated the end of the war in Europe in the city's streets and churches in May. Fighting in the Pacific however, did not end until August, following the atomic bombing of the Japanese cities of Hiroshima and Nagasaki.

✻ Canadiens superstar Maurice Richard made hockey history by scoring 50 goals in 50 games during the 1944-45 season. It was 17 years before it was done again – by "Boom Boom" Geoffrion.

1946

✻ Jackie Robinson made history when he joined the Montreal Royals, a farm team for the Brooklyn Dodgers, and became the first black to play professional baseball.

✻ In April, millionaire chemist and McGill professor Raymond Boyer was charged with espionage and released on $15,000 bail. At Boyer's trial in 1947, Igor Gouzenko testified that Russian spies were trying to undermine democratic countries. Gouzenko's revelations about Boyer and others helped fuel the Red

Scare of the late 1940s and 1950s. Boyer was sentenced to two years in jail.

✻ In June, Fred Rose, Labour-Progressive party MP, was sentenced to six years in prison for passing secret information to Russia.

✻ On December 4, Premier Maurice Duplessis charged that members of the Jehovah's Witnesses were spreading propaganda and attempting to convert Catholics. Several people were arrested and the liquor license of Crescent Street restaurant owner Frank Roncarelli, who posted bail for the group, was cancelled. In this celebrated civil-rights case, the Supreme Court in 1959 levied damages against Duplessis personally. Roncarelli's lawyer was Frank R. Scott.

1947

✻ The original Montreal Alouettes football team was organized. The game had been played in Montreal since 1865 when the first account of a game played in Canada recorded a match between English officers and civilians, mostly from McGill University. The Grey Cup, donated by Governor-General Lord Grey in 1909, was first won by the Alouettes in 1949, under coach Lew Hayman. It was won again under coach Sam Etcheverry in 1970 and under coach Marv Levy in 1974 and 1977.

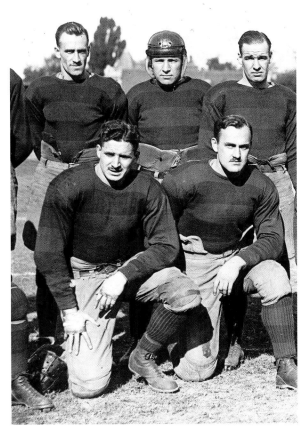

Men of Montreal's gridiron in 1931. The Alouettes football team wouldn't be formed until 1947. (GAZETTE FILES)

1948

✻ A manifesto, the Refus Global, was signed by a group of artists led by Paul-Émile Borduas, calling for rebellion against the "corruption" of the Roman Catholic Church and for liberation from society's strictures.

1949

✻ Most of this century in Montreal, as in Canada, has belonged to the Liberals, both provincially and federally. It was under Louis St. Laurent's leadership in 1949 and 1953 that the Liberals recorded their greatest victories.

1950

✻ Gérard Pelletier and Pierre Elliott Trudeau published the first edition of Cité Libre, dedicated to liberal democratic ideals in Quebec. The activist intel-

lectuals decried the Quebec government's nationalist and conservative policies.

1952

✻ In September, the CBC opened its first TV station in Canada in Montreal. CBFT broadcast in French and English, in black and white only.

1953

✻ Paul-Émile Léger, ordained a Sulpician priest in 1929 and named archbishop of Montreal in 1950, was consecrated as a cardinal. In 1967, he gave up the position to do missionary work in Africa.

1954

✻ Jean Drapeau won the mayoralty race against Camillien Houde. Drapeau was defeated in 1957 but was returned to power as head of the Montreal Civic Party in 1960. Drapeau would serve as mayor for 29 years in all. He stepped down in 1986 for what he said were health reasons. Drapeau died in August 1999.

Poet Emile Nelligan wrote some of the most cherished lines in the canon of Canadian verse before a mental breakdown in his early 20s confined him to a psychiatric institution for the rest of his life. He died in 1941. (GAZETTE FILES)

Montreal has been fertile ground for Liberal politicians for most of the 20th century. Here Prime Minister Louis St. Laurent takes his grand-nephew Bernard for a stroll in 1954. Bernard would grow up to become a prominent Quebec political journalist for the CBC. (GAZETTE FILES)

St. Laurent's wife, Jeanne, is greeted by sisters at Villa Maria as she arrives for a 1949 reception. (GAZETTE FILES)

Canadienne opened at the Gaiety Theatre. The play was Jean Anouilh's L'Alouette and an English version, The Lark, followed. The troupe was founded in 1957 by Gratien Gélinas for the production of plays in French and English.

1955

✳ On March 17, hockey fans rioted in Montreal to protest the suspension of Canadiens' hockey great Maurice Richard. Clarence Campbell, president of the National Hockey League, was pelted with food in the stands at the Forum and angry fans smashed windows on Ste. Catherine Street. One hundred people were arrested.

1957

✳ On October 18, the Montreal Herald newspaper, founded in 1811, shut down. Featured on the front page of the Herald's last edition was a photo of Maurice Richard scoring his 499th goal.

1958

✳ The first performance of the Comédie-

1959

✳ Marie-Marguerite d'Youville, founder of the Order of the Sisters of Charity (commonly known as the Grey Nuns) in Montreal, was beatified. She was the first Canadian-born person to be so honoured.
✳ On June 26, the St. Lawrence Seaway was officially opened by Queen Elizabeth, Prime Minister John Diefenbaker and U.S. President Dwight D. Eisenhower. Fifteen thousand watched as the ribbon was cut at the St. Lambert lock.
✳ On August 30, Montreal streetcars ran for the last time. Streetcars had been in use in Montreal since 1892.

1960

✳ Dorval's international airport officially opened in December. It cost $30 million. The big complaint was that the walk to board planes was too long.

1961

* The first public meeting of the Rassemblement pour l'Indépendance Nationale was held in Montreal. About 500 listened to speeches advocating Quebec's secession from Canada.
* In a December by-election, Claire Kirkland-Casgrain became the first woman to be elected to the Quebec National Assembly. Liberal Premier Jean Lesage immediately named her to cabinet. Voters in the Liberal stronghold Jacques-Cartier riding, who had elected her father Charles-Aimé Kirkland since 1939, re-elected Kirkland-Casgrain in the 1962 general election.

1962

* The Champlain Bridge, spanning the St. Lawrence, opened. The six-lane toll bridge cost $30 million. Tolls were discontinued in 1990.
* Place Ville Marie opened in September. American real estate legend William Zeckendorf, who built the United Nations building in New York City, began the project in 1955. The $80-million tower, built in the form of a cross, was a symbol of moderism in downtown Montreal and has been a landmark ever since.

1963

* On April 21, a 65-year-old security guard at a Canadian Army recruiting centre, Wilfred Vincent O'Neill, was killed when a bomb exploded there. Police suspected the terrorist Front de Libération du Québec. O'Neill's was the first of seven deaths, culminating in Pierre Laporte's in 1970, attributed to the FLQ. Georges Schoeters, Gabriel Hudon and Raymond Villeneuve were sentenced to 12 years each in the case; two other men received terms of 10 and six years. By the end of 1967, all had been paroled.
* In May, a series of FLQ bombs exploded in Westmount mailboxes. Army bomb expert Walter Leja was severely injured.
* André Laurendeau, a Montreal journalist and former leader of the anti-conscription and nationalist political party, Bloc Populaire, was named co-chairman of the Royal Commission on Bilingualism and Biculturalism. He was at Le Devoir for 21 years, the last 10 serving as editor. Until his death in 1968, Laurendeau pursued the challenge of finding a long-term solution that would provide constitutional equality for French- and English-Canadians.

1964

* On July 1, the National Assembly passed Bill 16, which moved toward ending the legal incapacity of married women. Under the changes, women no longer needed their husband's signature to transact business and they were given legal rights previously denied them, such as the ability to launch a lawsuit or act as the executor of a will. For years after 1964, however, bank managers and department stores in

Pierre Péladeau (seated) began publishing Le Journal de Montréal in 1964 and by the end of the century, the tabloid had the biggest circulation of any Quebec newspaper and was the flagship of the Quebecor publishing empire. (LE JOURNAL DE MONTRÉAL FILES)

The Portuguese vessel Braga steams into the recently opened St. Lawrence Seaway in 1961. Inaugurated in 1959, the seaway opened the Great Lakes to maritime shipping. (GAZETTE FILES)

Cardinal Paul-Émile Léger, the first Montreal cleric elevated to the Roman Catholic church's College of Cardinals, joined Mayor Jean Drapeau in 1966 for an inaugural ride on the city's recently completed Métro subway system. Characteristically at Drapeau's elbow was city Executive Comittee chairman Lucien Saulnier, the man who tempered the mayor's visions down to practicalities. It was Saulnier who persuaded Drapeau to go with an underground Métro system instead of the monorail skytrain the mayor originally favoured. (MONTREAL STAR – ALLAN LEISHMAN)

Quebec still refused to conduct business with women without their husbands' signature.
✻ Le Journal de Montréal, the flagship newspaper of Pierre Péladeau's publishing empire, Quebecor, began publication in June.

1966

✻ Montreal's rubber-tired subway system opened in October. The network, called the métro, as in Paris, consisted of 22.5 kilometres of lines and 26 stations. Other lines and stations were added later.

1967

✻ Expo 67 opened on April 27 and 50 million people – a record for any world's fair – eventually visited the site. Pavilions and exhibits were set up by 61 national and 22 private participants.
✻ On July 24, President Charles de Gaulle, visiting Montreal for Expo 67, stood on a balcony at city hall before a crowd of 10,000 and cried "Vive le Québec libre!" Twenty-three years earlier, he had stood on a balcony at the Windsor Hotel and declared "Vive le Canada." On July 26, he returned to France after Prime Minister Lester Pearson described his interference as unacceptable.

1968

✻ Canada's first heart-transplant operation was performed at the Montreal Heart Institute. Albert

Sgt.-Maj. Walter Leja, an army bomb disposal expert, lay critically injured on Westmount Boulevard moments after a mailbox bomb placed by the Front de Libération du Québec exploded in his hands on May 17, 1963. The FLQ had planted 15 dynamite bombs in Westmount mailboxes that day, of which five exploded in the early hours of the morning. Sgt.-Maj. Leja, who survived with crippling injuries, had already defused two other bombs that day. (Gazette – Garth Pritchard)

Murphy, a 58-year-old grocer from Chomedey, was the world's 18th heart-transplant patient. Murphy lived less than two days after the operation.

✳ In June, scores of people were injured when separatist-led rioting erupted while Prime Minister Pierre Trudeau reviewed the St. Jean Baptiste parade. Trudeau was not hurt but many others were injured when demonstrators hurled bottles and police charged the crowd.

✳ In September, tension over language exploded on the streets of St. Léonard. Angry members of the Italian community were protesting a plan by the local Catholic school commission to phase out English-language instruction. Their protest was met with violent rioting by 1,000 pro-French demonstrators demanding French-only education in Quebec. The Ligue pour l'Intégration Scolaire, whose leaders included Raymond Lemieux and Jacques Rose, wanted to keep English-language instruction out of Quebec. About 50 demonstrators were arrested.

✳ The first government lottery was created in Montreal by Jean Drapeau. He called it the voluntary tax; for $2 taxpayers could buy a chance to win a monthly $100,000 jackpot and other prizes totalling $25,000.

1969

✳ In February, radical students rampaged through Sir George Williams University's computer centre, destroying more than $1-million worth of equipment. The protest started over allegations of racial discrimination at the university.

✳ In March, thousands of demonstrators marched on McGill University demanding it be made a French-language university. It was called the "McGill Français" march.

✳ In May, Montreal's first civil marriage was performed.

✳ On October 7, Montreal police and firemen, demanding wage parity with their Toronto counterparts, walked off the job. Violence and looting erupted, striking taxi drivers attacked the Murray

The early 1970s were marked by several labour conflicts that resulted in violence but few were as bad as the clash that erupted on October 29, 1971 when more than 10,000 union activists demonstrating in support of La Presse workers clashed with police. (LE JOURNAL DE MONTRÉAL - JACQUES BOURDON)

Hill Limousine building, and one provincial police officer was killed. Later, troops and provincial police were called in.

✳ The Montreal Expos played their first game on April 14, cheered on by 29, 184 fans at Jarry Park.

1970

✳ The right to vote in Montreal municipal elections was extended to all adult residents. Previously, only property owners or tenants whose names appeared on leases could vote in municipal elections.

✳ On October 5, British trade commissioner James Cross was kidnapped by members of the FLQ, triggering what became known as the October Crisis. Quebec Labour Minister Pierre Laporte was kidnapped October 10 by another FLQ cell of which Paul and Jacques Rose were members, and later murdered. Jacques Rose was eventually convicted of being an accessory after the fact in Laporte's kidnapping. Paul was found guilty of kidnapping and murder. Francis Simard was found guilty of murder and Bernard Lortie of kidnapping. During the

October Crisis, the federal government invoked the War Measures Act and hundreds of Montrealers were detained.

1972

✳ When Canada pulled together its best professional hockey players to face off against the Soviet Union's hockey elite, most Canadians believed the home team would crush the visitors easily. It didn't work out that way. The Russians won the first game in Montreal 7-3, shocking the national team and firing up fans like no other hockey series had. In the end, Canada claimed victory when Paul Henderson scored the winning goal in Moscow to take the eighth game 6-5. Canada had won four games to the Soviets' three, and had tied one. But the Russians also claimed victory of sorts – their players had scored 32 goals during the series compared with 29 for the Canadian team.

✳ Thirty-seven people died in the Blue Bird Café fire, deliberately set. Three men were sentenced to life in prison for the crime.

1973

✳ Thousands of Montrealers move every year. For most of the century, the traditional moving day was May 1 but in 1973, the Quebec Rental Board decreed the date to be July 1. The change was made to avoid disrupting the school year.

✳ In September, the Van Horne mansion on Sherbrooke St. was demolished, sparking outrage and sustained concern about Montreal's architectural heritage.

✳ On November 14, Dr. Henry Morgantaler was acquitted of abortion charges by a jury that deliberated for 10 hours before reaching its verdict. Morgentaler was also acquitted in two subsequent trials and continues to operate clinics across Canada. There is no longer an abortion law in Canada.

1975

✳ On October 4, a new airport opened at Mirabel. The controversial facility, a white elephant from the start, cost half a billion dollars. Designed for international commercial flights, the airport lasted about 20 years before it was closed to all but cargo and charter flights.

✳ The Institut de microbiologie et d'hygiène de Montréal was renamed after Dr. Armand Frappier, who founded the institute in 1938.

1976

✳ Only the steel frame of the geodesic dome, built as the United States pavillion for Expo 67, remained after fire destroyed the plexiglass shell. Workers operating an acetylene torch accidentally started the fire. No one was hurt.

✳ On July 17, Queen Elizabeth opened the Montreal Olympic Games.

✳ On November 15, the Parti Québécois celebrated its first election victory at the Paul Sauvé Arena and in the streets of Montreal.

1977

✳ Bill 101, the French Language Charter, imposed restrictions on the use of English in the workplace and on commercial signs, and restricted access to

The election of René Lévesque's Parti Québécois on November 15, 1976 altered politics in Montreal, Quebec and Canada as no other event did in this century. (Le Journal de Montréal Files)

The Montreal Citizens' Movement, with Jean Doré at the helm, was swept to power in Montreal's 1986 civic election with the support of 68 per cent of voters. (LE JOURNAL DE MONTRÉAL - ANDRÉ VIAU)

English-language education. Quebec's language laws, designed to favour francophones and their language in Quebec, caused tens of thousands of people and companies to leave Montreal in the decade that followed.

1979

✳ On September 25, the Montreal Star newspaper shut down after 110 years of publication. It had been founded in 1869 by Hugh Graham who entered the peerage as Baron Atholstan in 1917 after his Montreal home was bombed by anti-conscription demonstrators. The newspaper was bought in 1925 by J. W. McConnell, who also controlled St. Lawrence Sugar Refineries. The folding of the Star was one of several newspaper closings across Canada that led to a commission of inquiry.

1980

✳ Quebecers voted against sovereignty-association in a referendum on May 20. About 85 per cent of eligible voters turned out; 59.6 per cent, including a majority of French-speaking Quebecers, voted No and 40.4 per cent voted Yes.

1982

✳ Alliance Quebec was formed by English-speaking community groups to defend minority rights in the province. At its founding convention, president Eric Maldoff offered to finance court challenges of Quebec law that banned the use of English from public signs.

1983

✳ Montreal held its first Fête des Neiges since 1889. The city had staged seven spectacular winter carnivals in the 1880s but attempts to continue the tradition into the 20th century were scuttled by leaders of the Board of Trade, the Grand Trunk Railway and the Canadian Pacific Railway, which were trying to attract immigrants to Canada. Winter carnivals, the two rail companies declared in The Gazette, "advertise the Dominion to the world as a place where the frost king reigns supreme most of the year."

1984

✳ Montreal lawyer Brian Mulroney was sworn in as Canada's 18th prime minister after leading the Progressive Conservative Party to power in a general election. He was prime minister until 1993.

1985

✳ Parti Québécois leader René Lévesque, premier since 1976, announced his resignation late in the evening of June 20. The PQ, led by Pierre Marc Johnson, was defeated in a December election by Robert Bourassa's Liberals.

1987

✳ On July 14, the city was flooded by a torrential rainstorm, resulting in one death on the Décarie Expressway.
✳ On November 1, René Lévesque died at his Montreal home.

1988

✳ The Supreme Court struck down parts of Bill 101 that ban languages other than French from com-

Montrealers have moved a lot in this century. With the highest percentage of rental occupancy of any city in the country, and a system whereby leases expire on a standard date (first May 1, later July 1) moving day has long been a major annual event. In the 1920s and 30s, as shown by these shots of moving day in the city's east end, every type of conveyance was pressed into service. (GAZETTE FILES – MONTREAL STAR)

mercial signs. Thousands rallied in Montreal to urge the Bourassa government to maintain the language restrictions. The Bourassa government reacted by invoking the notwithstanding clause of the constitution to pass Bill 178, which maintained the ban. ✷ After the Supreme Court ruled, someone set fire to the Alliance Quebec offices. The culprit was never caught.

1989

✷ On December 6, lone gunman Marc Lépine went on a killing rampage at the École Polytechnique of

The sign says, "Until next time," but René Lévesque would not live to fight another referendum after the one he lost in 1980, though he was re-elected premier the following year. (GAZETTE FILES)

the Université de Montréal. After singling out women, he killed 14 of them, then committed suicide. Tougher gun-control measures were adopted by Canada as a result.

✻ Phyllis Lambert of the Bronfman family opened the Canadian Centre for Architecture in the old Shaughnessy mansion on what was once Dorchester Boulevard. Lambert has long been active in protecting Montreal's heritage buildings and promoting education about the city's architectural past.

1990

✻ On July 10, provincial police were called in to dismantle a road block that had been set up in March by members of the Mohawk band at Kanesatake near Oka. Mohawks were protesting plans to expand a golf course on disputed land. The police operation erupted into violence, with one officer killed, and the dispute escalated into a standoff that dragged on all summer. In a show of support, Kahnawake Mohawks blocked the Mercier Bridge. After several weeks, the army was called and finally, on August 27, the barricades came down. In the end, the federal government agreed to buy the disputed 39-hectare parcel of land and transfer it to the band.

✻ Jean-Paul Lemieux, one of Montreal's greatest and most popular artists, died at the age of 86.

1992

✻ Concordia University professor Valery Fabrikant killed three fellow professors in the downtown Henry Hall Building and a fourth victim died later in hospital. Fabrikant was sentenced to life in prison with no chance of parole before 25 years.

✻ On December 27, provincial legislation was passed to allow extended shopping hours during the week and on Sunday.

1993

✻ The Montreal Canadiens won the Stanley Cup – the 24th time – but celebrations were disrupted when hooligans rampaged along Ste. Catherine Street, looting stores. One hundred and fifteen people were arrested and 168, including 49 police officers, suffered minor injuries. Similar rioting had erupted after the Habs won the Stanley Cup in 1986.

✻ In October, Montreal's $95-million casino, the largest in Canada, opened in the former French pavilion on Île Notre Dame. By the end of the century, gambling and lotteries were bringing in more than $1 billion a year in profits for the Quebec government.

1994

✳ A provincial inquiry headed by retired judge Albert Malouf called the 4,500-member Montreal police force poorly trained, discriminatory and badly supervised.
✳ In December, Quebec's most successful singing star of the century, Céline Dion, married René Angelil in the Notre Dame Basilica. It was the closest Montreal would come to a royal wedding.

1995

✳ Quebecers voted No in a second sovereighty referendum. The results were tight, with 50.6 per cent voting No and 49.4 voting Yes to giving the Parti Québécois government the power to declare Quebec's independence. In a speech, Premier Jacques Parizeau singled out "money and ethnic votes" as being to blame for the loss.

1996

✳ Robert Bourassa, former provincial Liberal leader and premier from 1970–76 and 1985–1994, died in Montreal after a battle with cancer. He was 63.

1997

✳ Pierre Péladeau, head of the Quebecor printing and publishing empire, died in hospital at 72.

1998

✳ It was called the Ice Storm of the Century – five days of freezing rain in the dead of winter fell on Montreal and southwestern Quebec, eastern Ontario, the Maritimes and the northeastern U.S. Hydro towers crumpled under the weight of the ice. Thousands of Montreal-area homes and businesses were blacked out for up to nine days. Off the Island, blackouts lasted for up to 33 days. More than 20 people died as a result of the storm.

1999

✳ Montreal's longest-serving mayor, Jean Drapeau, died on August 12 at age 83.

Pierre Trudeau helped inspire the federalist victory in the 1980 sovereignty referendum.
(GAZETTE FILES)

One of Quebec's leading painters of the century, Jean-Paul Lemieux, rendered here in characteristic self-portrait. (GAZETTE FILES)

Phyllis Lambert, daughter of distillery magnate Sam Bronfman, founded the internationally reputed Canadian Centre for Architecture in Montreal. She has been a champion of both modern design and the preservation of Montreal's architectural heritage. (GAZETTE – PETER MARTIN)

Quebec pop diva Céline Dion married René Angelil in 1994. (GAZETTE – GORDON BECK)

The maple leaf flag borne by members of the crowd at the giant Canadian unity rally in the final nervous days of the 1995 sovereignty referendum was larger than the stage. An estimated 100,000 people from all parts of the country gathered in front of Montreal's Place du Canada on October 27 for what is believed to be the biggest political rally in Canadian history. GAZETTE – GORDON BECK)

✳ Céline Dion performed a record-breaking stadium tour in Europe – 180,000 in Paris, a sell-out crowd of 75,000 in Brussels and 122,000 in London.

✳ The Cirque du Soleil's yellow and blue tent went up in the St. Michel district of Montreal for the opening of its *Dralion* show. The Cirque also opened two shows in other cities, including the new water-based show, *O*, in Las Vegas.

✳ Sébastien Lareau became the first Canadian to win a U.S. Open tennis title when he and partner Alex O'Brien won the men's doubles championship.

✳ The hot summer was celebrated with a string of festivals and events enjoyed by hundreds of thousands of people, establishing Montreal once again as one of the best festival cities of the world. ◆

End-of-century Montreal is one of the best and liveliest festival cities in the world, as this photo of a street show during the Jazz Festival attests. (Le Journal de Montréal - Luc Laforce)